LETTERS

LETTERS

LULLUS OF MAINZ

Copyright 2006 by Dalcassian Press

All rights reserved. No part of this book may be reproduced in any manner whatsoever without written permission except in the case of brief quotations embodied in critical articles and reviews.

No part of this publication may be reproduced, distributed, or transmitted in any form or by any means, including photocopying, recording, or other electronic or mechanical methods, without the prior written permission of the publisher, except in the case of brief quotations embodied in critical reviews and certain other non-commercial uses permitted by copyright law. For permission request, write to Dalcassian Press at admin@thescriptoriumproject.com

Translator: Curtin, D.P. (1985-)

ISBN: 979-8-3493-7795-2 (Paperback)
ISBN: 979-8-3493-7791-4 (eBook)
Library of Congress Control Number:

Printed by Ingram Content Group, 1 Ingram Blvd, La Vergne, Tennessee
First Printing 2006, Dalcassian Press, Wilmington, DE

This work is part of a series produced in association with the Scriptorium Project and its community of scholars and translators.
Please visit our website at: www.thescriptoriumproject.com

LATIN TEXT

EPISTOLA PRIMA. LULLUS DALHUNO. (Anno Domini 752.)

Reverendissimo fratri Dalhuno, jam dudum magistro Lullus indignus diaconus, sine praerogativa meritorum diaconatus officio fungens, optabilem in Domino salutem.

Almitatis tuae clementiam intimis precibus flagito, ut meae mediocritatis carinam fulcire digneris tuis almis oraminibus, quatenus tuarum orationum intercessionibus, seu pelta protectus, ad portum salutis pervenire merear, et piaculorum meorum in hoc terreno ergastulo veniam consequi, sicut jam praeterito anni circulo, per Denewaldum fratrem nostrum, litterarum mearum portitorem, deprecatus sum. Ergo vilium munusculorum transmissio schedulam istam comitatur non tam digna quam devota mente directa. Similiter obsecro ut mihi Aldhelmi episcopi aliqua opuscula seu prosarum, seu metrorum, aut rhythmicorum, dirigere digneris ad consolationem peregrinationis meae, et ob memoriam ipsius beati antistitis; et mihi per aliqua verba tuae affabilitatis, indica, quid de istis valeat precibus tua fraternitas perficere, quae inhianter audire satago. Bene valentem te et proficientem in prosperitate dierum, et intercedentem pro me exopto longis temporibus.

Fama est fictilibus coenasse Agathoclea regem.
Atque abacum Samio saepe onerasse luto.
Fercula gemmatis cum poneret aurea vasis,
Et misceret opes pauperiemque simul.
Quaerenti causam respondit: Rex ego qui sum
Sicaniae, figulo sum genitore satus.
Fortunam reverenter habe, quicunque repente
Dives ab exiguo progrediere loco.

EPISTOLA II. INGALICE LULLO. (Anno Domini 752.)

Claro atque charissimo Dei ministro Lullo Ingalice, indignus presbyter tuus, tamen per omnia devotus famulus in Domino optabilem salutem.

Litterae namque prudentiae tuae et munera targitatis tuae ad me usque directa pervenerunt, quibus diligenter lectis et consideratis, post praemissam pacificam salutationem, si bene intellexi, insinuasti nobis erga vos diversas molestias et tribulationes, quae saepe solent in hoc mundo occupare servos Christi secundum Apostoli sententiam: Omnes, qui pie volunt vivere in Christo, persecutionem patiuntur; contraque omnia tentamenta, orationum nostrarum, qualiacunque sunt, adminicula humiliter postulasti; quod et omnis congregatio nostra pro vestra sospitate sedulo ad Dominum preces fundere studuit, et nunc, amantissime diacone, quia vicem rescribendo eruditionis tuae scriptis, propter parvitatem ingenioli mei, digne debitum persolvere non potui, tamen scio quia vera charitas omnia sustinet. Haec pauca verba rusticitatis meae cum minimis munusculis, id est, quatuor cultellos nostra consuetudine factos, et calamistrum argenteum, et mappam unam, per fidelem portitorem fratrem vestrum, imo nostrum Aldredum amabili praesentiae tuae tantum pro memoria charitatis transmittere curavi. Quaeso fraternitatem tuam ut eo animo a te haec suscipiantur, quo a me destinata noscuntur. Sed et intercessorem nostrum apud Deum, venerabilem Bonifacium praesulem, omnis caterva fratrum nostrorum cum abbaterio in Dei dilectione salutare desiderat.

EPISTOLA III. LULLUS LEOBGITHAE. (Circa annum Domini 752.)

Sorori in Christo charissimae Leobgythae Lullus exiguus servus, auctoritate domini Bonifacii discipulorum, in Domino salutem.

Non immemorem tuae sagacitatis industriam aestimo evangelicae sententiae qua dicitur: Beati pauperes spiritu, quoniam ipsorum est regnum coelorum. Illa paupertas patienter ferenda est, eodem evangelista testante, qui ait: In patientia vestra possidebitis animas vestras. Illud Davidici cum corde retinens, quia secundum multitudinem dolorum tuorum consolationes Dei laetificarunt animam tuam. Nec enim contemptui vel oblivioni tuam sinceram in Domino germanitatem deditam arbitreris, quamvis per interducias temporum corporali praesentia secernamur; neque in tuis necessitatibus fessum me esse ullo modo autumes, sed tantum diabolicae fraudis astutia praeoccupatum atque ministrorum ejus subdola insectatione fatigatum scias; et, juxta prophetae dictum: Taedet me vitae meae propter filios nequitiae. Quidquid autem necessitatibus tuis desit, per Gundwinum diaconum reversurum indicato, suggere illi ut in laboribus meis non lassescat, quia valde rarus est qui tribulationes meas mecum participare velit. Vale in Domino, intercedens pro me tanto enixius quanto graviore angustia deprimor.

EPISTOLA IV. LULLUS GREGORIO. (Anno Domini 752.)

Clarae Christi Ecclesiae lampadi luciferae, meoque in doctrina divinae legis devotissimo adjutori, Gregorio duplici presbyteratus abbatisque honore, cum praecedente propriorum meritorum suffragio, decorato, Lullus, extremus orthodoxae matris, videlicet Ecclesiae, alumnus, immarcescibilis charitatis, in angulari lapide utriusque testamenti, salutiferam salutem.

Fido gestante gerulo munera largitatis tuae ad me usque delata pervenerunt, sed et suavissimae benevolae charitatis tuae salutationes omne munus vincentes more solito pariter comitabantur, quibus auditis et perceptis, uberes Deo piissimo primitus egi gratias ut decuit; et deinde fraternitati tuae debitas reddidi grates, quia te in minore potestate fidelem sciebam, in majore citius fideliorem comprobavi. Comperto igitur prosperitatis tuae successu aeger animus utrumque egit: gaudebat de ascensione chari sodalis, sed contristabatur de divisione, quia hoc intolerabile apud homines videtur, dum is qui prae caeteris plus diligitur repente subtrahitur, quamvis pro certo sciam quod nulla terrarum spatia illos dividere possunt quos verus Christi amor indisrupto germanitatis vinculo nectit, teste Deo, ne videar adulando fallere, quia te, Pater, quantum mentis possibilitas attribuit, interni affectus amore diligo. Hoc autem subnixa prece humiliter obsecro, ut nunquam semel in Christo coeptam charitatem, desidia torporis, in nostro pectore frigescere sinamus, velut parvam scintillam tenuis ignis fulva cinerum favilla suffocatam, ne in derisum veniamus a praetereuntibus coeptum aedificium considerantibus turris. Dicit Scriptura: Qui perseveraverit usque in finem, salvus erit, nec quilibet artifex de coepto opere laudatur, sed de perfecto. Hoc autem meam mediocritatem quamlibet aetate juniorem, merito graduque minorem, scientia inferiorem, absque ullo dubitationis scrupulo et servasse, et servaturam esse scito. De tua vero vitae gravitate, mentisque stabilitate nihil dubito. Muniamus nos spirituali armatura juxta apostoli praeceptum: Orantes pro invicem ut salvemur, quia multum deprecatio justi assidua, Jacobo attestante, apud Deum valet; et eo diligentius huic insistamus, quo vehementius nos variis tentationum telis impugnari non ignoramus. Dextera scilicet fortior laevam infirmiorem adjuvare non cessat; et laeva dexterae, sicut ancilla dominae, deservire non desinet. Id est, meam instabilitatem bonae vitae tuae exemplis castigando, corrigendo, admonendo, quamvis absentem corpore, spiritu tamen praesentem, sicut tibi moris est, ad melioris vitae perfectionem deducere non desinas, et ego tibi humili devotione, quantum vires suppeditant, fidelem famulatum in omnibus praebebo. Exhortatoria mediocritatis meae verba, quamvis fatua et superflua videantur, obsecro ut non moleste a tuae charitatis collegio recipiantur, quae sola charitas exigebat scribere sine dictandi materia, quae omnia vincit, sicut scriptum est: Omnia vincit amor, et nos cedamus amori, ablata omni tumoris superbia. Haec sunt suasoria verba quae sine meo periculo dicere non possum, ut in hac temporali potestate et terrestri ditione, qua, auctore Deo, jam nunc uteris, dominicae sententiae semper memor sis sonantis: Regnum meum non est de hoc mundo; et illud apostoli: Nolite diligere mundum, neque ea quae in mundo sunt. Quibus verbis quid aliud innuitur, nisi aperte dixisse illum intelligamus: In illum nolite oculum mentis vestrae figere, quem quotidie ipsa ruina sua cernitis cadere, sed in illum tota mentis intentione aspicite, illumque totis viribus diligite, qui ante omnia saecula est, et per omnia saecula immutabilis manet, qui futuro et praeterito tempore caret, sed esse sibi semper essentialiter est. Quid est enim hujus mundi fugitiva felicitas, et caduca prosperitas, nisi vapor et fumus? Inter temporalem prosperitatem et aeternam felicitatem multum distare quis peritorum ignorat? Discamus igitur hac temporali potestate frui praeter aeternam felicitatem, et in cujus comparatione nobis omnia vilescant. Vestimenta pretiosa, caballos farre pastos, accipitres, falconesque cum curvis unguibus, latrantes canes, scurrarum bacchationes, cibi potusque exquisitae dulcedinis saporis, argenti aurique rutilantis pondera spernamus, ne sit mollis culcitrae pausatio, molliaque cervicalia a viris potius exhibeantur, quam a flammeis puellis. Ante omnia, incauta familiaritas extranearum feminarum abscindatur, quia saepe seducimur incauta securitate pejus quam aperta tentatione. Tumultuosam ministrorum multitudinem clandestina divinarum Scripturarum eloquia expellant, quia illa fovea omni custodia cavenda est, per quam plurimos miserabili ruina conspicimus corruisse. Nam saepe robustus miles infestissima telorum jaculatione eo fortius impugnatur, quo invictus videtur. Quamvis hoc inisse te negotium liquido noverim occasione lucrandarum animarum, et pro studio multiplicius serviendi Deo, tamen memento quia mollem manum durus capulus exasperat. Quapropter, chare collega, jam dudum, et nunc pie praeceptor, in omnibus operibus tuis memorare novissima tua, et in aeternum non peccabis. Festinatio autem ad te veniendi, propter multiplicem tribulationem, quam jugiter, Deo gratias, sustinemus, mihi undique denegata est. Hujus muneris magnitudinem noli intendere, sed devotam mentem dirigentis intuere. Antiquae familiaritatis fiducia freto libet mihi haec epistiuncula quamdam sententiam frequenter apud nos habitam, quando limpida dicta Dei communiter rimabamur, breviter tangere, nequaquam tamen ad tuae purae religionis personam pertinentem, cujus bene recordaris dum legitur, sed ad quemdam schismaticum nefandissimum pertinebat, qui semper jurare solebat nihil se terreni accepturum. Cum subito ex improviso, velut novum phantasma, episcopus apparuit, hoc jam maxima ex parte futurum esse formidabo. Longioris sermonis prolixitas legenti fastidium ne gignat (nam sapiens paucis utitur verbis, stultus autem multis fatigatur, sicut et ego), obsecro, istius epistolae rubiginem emendando absterge, meique erroris indulgentia detur. Deus tibi, quod ad salutem tuam pertineat, clementer inspirare dignetur; et cum grege tibi commisso incolumem Pastor pastorum te custodiat. Propria manu scripsi haec. Observa quae praecipiuntur et salvus eris.

EPISTOLA V. LULLUS DENEARDO ET ALIIS. (Anno Domini 755.)

Charissimis filiis Denehardo, Eanbertho, Winberto, Sigeherio, Sigewaldo, Lullus antistes in Domino salutem.

Admonemus vos ut rogetis omnes ubique Deo servientes, tam servos Dei quam ancillas Christi in provincia Thuringorum, universamque plebem, ut in communi misericordiam Domini deprecentur, quatenus ab imminenti pluviarum flagello liberemur; id est, ut unam hebdomadam abstineant se ab omni carne, et ab omni potu in quo mel sit; secunda feria, quarta feria, et sexta feria jejunetis usque ad vesperum; et unusquisque servorum Dei et sanctimonialium quinquaginta psalmos cantet omni die in illa septimana, et illas missas, quae pro tempestatibus fieri soleant, celebrare vos, presbyteri, recordamini. Misimus vobis nomina domini Romani episcopi, pro quo unusquisque vestrum XXX missas cantet et illos psalmos, et jejunium juxta constitutionem nostram. Similiter pro duobus laicis nomine Megenfrido, et Rabano X missas unusquisque vestrum cantet. Valete in Domino semper.

EPISTOLA VI. ALREDUS ET OSGIVA LULLO. (Anno Domini 755.)

Alredus rex et Osgiva regina Lullo venerabili episcopo nobis perpetuali amicitia copulato in Christo salutem.

Scripta beatitudinis tuae simul cum muneribus litteris assignatis debita gratulationis reverentia suscepimus, maximasque omnipotenti Deo egimus gratias, quod te in tam longa peregrinatione desudantem, et in Christi agonibus decertantem, optatae conservavit sospitati; et ideo revertentibus venerabilibus viris, gaudium nostrum, sacrorum apicum attestatione, signamus, ac petimus uti quotidianis orationibus episcopatus tuus studium ac votum suum circa salutem nostram dignetur impendere. Nos quoque simul cum nominibus nostrorum amicorum, et propinquorum, quae hic subscripta sunt, litterarum custodia facias contineri, orationibusque et missarum celebrationibus perpetuis Dei patrociniis commendemur. Eodemque modo de vobis, et de nominibus ad nos delatis, secundum vestram petitionem, facere curabimus, ut in cunctis monasteriis nostris ditionibus subjunctis perpetuis litterarum monumentis commendentur, et orationum subsidiis Deo quotidie praesententur. Illudque pietati nostrae satis placuisse cognosce, quod sanctimonia tua de Ecclesiarum aut populi perturbatione sollicita est, quae etiam ut fierent, Dei aliquo dispensationis consilio credimus esse provisa. Nostris quoque, dilectissime frater, legationibus ad dominum vestrum gloriosissimum regem Carl. obsecramus, consulendo subvenias, ut pax et amicitia, quae omnibus conveniunt, facias stabiliter inter nos confirmari.

Divina majestas indefesso certamine pro Christi Ecclesia desudantem te conservare dignetur.

Parva munuscula tuae dignitati admisimus, id est duodecim sagos, cum annulo aureo majori dono ad dotem.

EPISTOLA VII. PIPPINUS LULLO. (Anno Domini 755)

Pippinus gratia Dei rex Francorum vir illuster domino sancto Patri Lullo episcopo.

Cognitum scimus sanctitati vestrae qualem pietatem et misericordiam Deus fecit praesenti anno in terra ista. Dedit tribulationem pro delictis nostris; post tribulationem autem magnam atque mirabilem consolationem, sive abundantiam fructus terrae, quem modo habemus. Est ob hoc, atque pro aliis causis nostris opus est nobis illi gratias agere, quia dignatus est servos suos consolari per ejus misericordiam. Sic nobis videtur ut, absque jejunio indicto, unusquisque episcopus in sua parochia litanias faciat, non cum jejunio, nisi tantum in laude Dei, qui talem nobis abundantiam dedit, et faciat unusquisque homo suas eleemosynas et pauperes pascat. Et sic praevidere faciatis, et ordinare de verbo nostro, ut unusquisque homo, aut vellet aut nollet, suam decimam donet. Valete in Christo.

EPISTOLA VIII. MAGINGOZ LULLO. (Anno Domini 755.)

Sacerdoti Christi magnifico, reverentia pariter et amore non mediocriter amplectendo, Lullo episcopo Magingoz, servus servorum Dei, perennem in Domino salutem.

Aperto Scripturarum divinarum testimonio declaratur veritatem esse Dominum Salvatorem, ac de ipso dictum esse per prophetam: Quaerite faciem ejus semper, quam ob rem solutionem quaestionis alicujus quae videlicet infirmitatis nostrae cognitioni facilis non est, a dignationis vestrae largitate id ipsum flagitantes multum desideramus accipere. Itaque constitutio matrimonii Christianorum in jungendo, vel separando, a Patribus tanta diversitate nobis videtur disponi, ut vix una et compar sententia ipsorum, nostrae pateat parvitati. Videntur namque concorditer Isidorus ac Hieronymus affirmare non debere adulteram teneri a viro, cui sociata, (0825B)alteri se, more meretricis, adjungat, utpote quae unam carnem nefarie dividens, indignam se et alienam ab honore connubii divinitus instituti reddiderit, et hoc esse praeceptum et permissum a Salvatore, cum uxorem non dimittendam absque fornicationis causa praeciperet. Augustinus vero cum sententiam eamdem Salvatoris diuturna tractatione ventilasset, nihil planae elucidationis, certe nostrae omnino teneritudini captabile, profert; sed hoc in extremo dicebat, quia quomodo praeceptum hoc Salvatoris accipi debuisset, late operosissimam adhuc superesse quaestionem, commemorans vero mulierem ab accusatione Judaeorum a Domino liberatam dicit: Non male illi vir mulieri licet in adulterium lapsae conciliaretur. Beatus vero Leo papa feminam, capto ab hostibus marito, cogente solitudine, inculpabiliter alteri posse copulari cum desperaretur captus, et reverso forte priore, separatam a posteriore, principali restitui dicit; ubi notandum videtur quod statim destitutae conjugi nubendi licentiam tribuit. Apud Isidorum vero vel Hieronymum proditio foederis conjugalis matrimonium separat. Quid ergo supersit conjugi quem, vel quam, solitudo perurget, si et Isidori vel Hieronymi ac Leonis decretum juste creditur esse tenendum, nisi ut se matrimonio conjungat alterius, me fateor ignorare. Bonitatis igitur vestrae dignationem, per charitatem qua Christus Dominus semper ubique membra sua sibi copulare probatur obsecramus, ut ignorantiam nostram (0825D)ac dubitationem, sic Domino possibilitatem largiente, illuminare dignemini, ut audire a remuneratore perpetuo mereamini: Euge, serve bone, etc.

EPISTOLA IX. MAGINGOZ LULLO. (Circa annum Domini 755.)

Domino in Christo summopere venerando Lullo episcopo Magingoz optabilem supplex in Domino sempiternae beatitudinis salutem.

Scit plane sublimitatis vestrae prudentia quia contra discrimina maxima consiliorum adjutoriis et integris et ex omni parte solidatis modis omnibus opus est. Notum vero fieri venerandae charitatis vestrae dignationi desideramus quia exitum sororis nostrae extremum spiritum agentis, moeroribus ac timoribus undique depressi, praestolamur, mortem videlicet carnis illius, instinctu naturalis conditionis, velut propria delentes, et pro animae illius eventu incerto, et soli judici piissimo noto, et insuper familiae loci illius tenerrimae, et propemodum, sine ulla consilii firmitate, discissionem, vel (quod gravissimum est) animarum interitum pertimescentes. Quapropter magnitudinis vestrae pietati humili intentione supplicantes obsecramus per Christum Salvatorem resurrectionemque mortuorum, uti nobis supradictis cruciatibus afflictis quid post obitum illius sit pro stabilitate salutari monasterioli faciendum, prout, Domino juvante, colligere valeatis, litteris indicare per hunc nuntium non dedignemini. Sunt enim, sicut scitis, illic filiae fratris nostri velatae, in quas fortasse intentio ignorantium conversa est; sed nulla ex his adhuc vel aetate, vel sensus aliqua firmitate, ad suscipiendum tale pondus congrua poterit judicari. Et formidamus dispersionem inconsultam familiae, nisi celeriter ordo ac stabilitas per abbatissam collocetur. Nec tamen vel intra cellulam, vel intrinsecus nos posse reperire credimus per quam vel verbo ac specie tenus valeat cohaerere, praeter puellulas quas diximus, quibus maximum periculum suscipientibus, et nobis fortasse persuadentibus, formidamus. Quapropter iterata supplicatione per Christum Salvatorem obsecramus, ut nobis quod saluberrimum inter hujusmodi necessitates fieri credatis (nobis revelare celeritate qua diximus nec dedignemini nec gravemini.

Valere beatitudinem vestram, et in Christo magis ac magis pro nobis intercedentes proficere integris certisque nisibus cordis optamus, officio Lulloni episcopo.

EPISTOLA X. LULLUS PAPAE. (Circa annum Domini 755.)

Sancta, et regularia instituta canonica auctoritate confirmata tam episcoporum nostrorum venerabilium, quam etiam domini nostri regis Pippini, consiliatorumque ejus, manifesta ratione scimus conservanda. Quapropter charitati vestrae reticere non audemus quod in parochiam nostram, contra jus canonicum, (0826D)a Willefrido presbytero quidam adductus est presbyter in alia ordinatus parochia, non consentiente antecessore meo sancto Bonifacio archiepiscopo, neque me successore ejus, qui et institutionis vestrae decreta contemnens, et in parochia nostra constitutus nostrum sprevit magisterium. Cognita enim canonum auctoritate, decrevistis ut omnes presbyteri qui in parochia sunt sub potestate episcopi esse debeant, et ut nullus eorum praesumat in ejus parochia aut baptizare, aut missas celebrare, sine jussione episcopi, et ut omnes presbyteri ad concilium episcopi conveniant: quae omnia facere contempsit praedictus ille presbyter nomine Enred; et ideo secundum quod definistis, increpationis a me sententiam sortitus est. Sed cum nec ita emendatus poenitere de praeteritis voluit, novissime, secundum canonicam institutionem vestram, excommunicatus est a me, et exinde a supradicto Willefrido susceptus est ac defensus. Vestra autem nunc de his charitas quod rectum sit ac justum judicet, et non solum de his, sed de omnibus quae perverse male vivendo peregit, et hic manifestata reperiuntur. Abstulit enim mancipia et servos de ecclesiis sibi commissis, Faegenolphum servum nostrum, et duos filios ejus Raegenolphum et Amanolphum, et uxorem ejus Leobthruthe, et filiam ejus Amalthruthe, tradidit eos in Saxoniam, contra equum unum, homini nomine Huelp, quod ipse eos duxisset in Saxoniam. Willefridum vero supradicti Regenolphes filium transmisit ultra mare cum Enredo, et ipse eum dedit matri suae in servitutem. Servum vero et ancillam quos Aohtrich dedit ad ecclesias nostras pro anima filii sui, supradictus Willefridus abstulit atque rapuit furtim. Nomen servi Thecdo, et nomen uxoris ejus Aotlind; Liudo vero servum nostrum Enred presbyter tradidit puero Aldberchtes de Effernace nomen Upbit, contra equum unum; et Erpwine servum nostrum aliis nescientibus furtim nocte abstulit cum nonaginta et quatuor porcis, quem Hredun dedit ad ecclesiam nostram; et altera vice abstulit duos servos nostros Zeitolf et Zeizhelm, et primo quatuor boves nostros, secundo tres, et novissime octo vaccas cum septem bobus. Jumenta vero septem optima aetate quatuor annorum, quae dedit Wenilo ad ecclesias, supradictus Willefridus abstulit, et multos alios equos inde nutritos, quos minavit ad Hamulanburg. De auro vero et argento quod dedit Regenthryth filia Athuolphi ad ecclesias nostras, duas armillas aureas et quinque siglas aureas valentes pretio trecentorum solidorum, et aliorum fidelium virorum ac mulierum pretia Enred abstulit ab ecclesiis supradictis, non solum in auro et argento, sed etiam in vestimento, et armis, et equis. Sed quia longum est ut per ordinem replicemus omnia quae rapta sunt ecclesiis supradictis ac spoliatis, et quae facta contra canonica instituta sunt, vestro sanctissimo judicio ascribimus emendanda.

EPISTOLA XI. LULLUS OSWITHAE. (Circa annum Domini 755.)

Lullus exiguus atque humilis antistes Svithan ejusque subjectis.

Apostolicum praeceptum est, Oswitha, ut gregem Domini sollicite servando pascamus, ne absque ovili repertus, luporum morsibus pereat. Hoc quidem te egisse, et acturam esse confidens, quae a sanctissimo viro Bonifacio martyre Christi, ejusque discipulis, regularis vitae disciplinam suscepisti, putabam juxta modulum intelligentiae tuae; sed (quod tristis ac moerens dicere cogor) longe aliter fecisse comprobaris, quae, neglectis animabus, pro quibus Christus mortuus est, de quarum vita reddita es rationem in die judicii ante tribunal Christi, dum sacro palliatas feminas N. et N. contra statuta canonum, et sanctae regulae disciplinam, sine licentia et consilio meo, ac injuriam Dei, ejusque matris beatae Mariae semper virginis, cujus famulatum exhibere debuerunt, in laqueum diaboli propter arrogantiam ac voluptatem laicorum explendam, ad perditionem animarum suarum, liberas ire permiseris in longinquam regionem, non recolens illud evangelicum: Si caecus caeco ducatum praebet, ambo in foveam cadunt. Et illud: Anima quae peccaverit, ipsa morietur. Sed ne forte hanc meam objurgationem parvi pendens contemnas, apostolico te sermone percutiam, quo ait: Peccantes coram omnibus argue, ut caeteri timorem habeant. Pro hujusmodi stultitia excommunicatam te esse scias cum omnibus tuis qui hunc negligentiae reatum consentiendo perpetraverunt, usque dum digna satisfactione hanc emendetis culpam. Illas autem vagas et inobedientes supradictas feminas, intra cellam vestram non recipiatis, sed foras monasterium excommunicatae ab Ecclesia Christi sedeant, poenitentiam agentes, dum venerint, in pane et aqua, et vos similiter abstinendo ab omni carne, et omni potu qui melle indulcoratur, scientes quod si spernitis istam increpationem, quod spernatis eum qui a Deo missus est peccatores salvos facere, id est Christum, qui dixit in Evangelio: Qui vos spernit me spernit, qui autem me spernit spernit eum qui me misit, id est, Deum Patrem omnipotentem. Optamus in Christo ad meliora vos converti.

EPISTOLA XII. CUTHBERTUS LULLO. (Circa annum Domini 756.)

Reverendissimo fratri et in amore Christi charissimo Lullo coepiscopo, simulque cooperatoribus tuis episcopis et sacerdotibus Dei, quorum nomina in libro vitae scripta teneantur, Cuthbertus, servus servorum Dei, cum aliis consacerdotibus Christi et presbyteris seu abbatibus, aeternae prosperitatis ac pacis in Domino salutem.

Profitemur igitur, charissimi, sincerissima intentione coram Deo et electis angelis ejus, quia quandocunque vestram dilectionem pacis ac prosperitatis proventum et sanctae religionis in Christo profectum, sacraeque exhortationis fructum de aliorum conversatione abundantius habere, rumigerulis referentibus, audimus, quod inde satis gaudentes et pro vobis obnixius orantes laeti gratias agimus largitori bonorum omnium Deo. Quando igitur aliqua religioni vestrae injuria facta, aut aliquod irrogatum narratur damnum, moeror et tristitia nos cruciat, quia nimirum sicut gaudio vestro in Christo congaudemus, ita et adversitate pro Christo contristati compatimur. Non enim aliquando in memoria nostra oblitterari possunt diversi atque indefessi tribulationum angores quos, ut viscera nostra, vos ipsi cum Deo dilecto Patre nostro beatae memoriae Bonifacio martyre, inter persecutores paganos et haereticos, atque schismaticos seductores, in tam periculosa ac ferocitate plena peregrinatione, pro amore aeternae patriae, longo tempore, sustinebatis; et quia illo, scilicet per agonem martyrii, cum suis plurimis domesticis, ad aeternam coelestis patriae quietem gloriose feliciterque migrante, vos, qui superstites talium estis, forsitan eo periculosius ac difficilius inter diversa tentamenta conversamini, quo tanto Patre, et doctore ad praesens vos orbatos esse constat. Et quamvis hinc quaedam moestitiae amaritudo nostra discruciat valide praecordia, tamen hujusce doloris gemitum quaedam saepius ad memoriam rediens nimiae ac novae exsultationis hilaritas jucundat ac mitigat, dum frequentius recolentes, admirabili vel potius ineffabili Dei pietati tripudiantes gratias agimus, quod tam praeclarum, speculatorem coelestis bibliothecae, tamque egregium Christi militem, cum multis bene educatis et optime instructis discipulis, gens Anglorum advena, Britannia, meruit, palam omnibus, ad spirituales agones, et ad multarum, per Dei omnipotentis gratiam, salutem animarum, de sese procul laudabiliter emittere, ut longe lateque ferocissimas nationes per devia diutius errantes, de lata ac spatiosa voragine perditionis perpetuae ad splendifluas semitas supernae patriae, per sacrae exhortationis incitamenta, et per exempla pietatis ac bonitatis, ipse ductor et signifer antecedendo, et adversa quaeque, opitulante Deo, fortiter expugnando, feliciter perduceret, quod ita actutum veraciter fieri, etiam rerum effectus gloriosius quam dicta demonstrant; et in illis quoque locis, quos ante eum nullus aliquando, evangelizandi causa, doctor adire tentabat. Unde igitur post incomparabile toto orbe apostolicae electionis et numeri mysterium, aliorumque tunc temporis evangelizantium discipulorum Christi ministerium, hunc inter egregios et optimos orthodoxae fidei doctores et amabiliter habemus et laudabiliter veneramur. Unde in generali synodo nostra, ubi et de caeteris omnibus quae vestrae modo sanctitati paucis depromimus, plenius inter nos conferebamus, ejus diem natalitii, illiusque cohortis cum eo martyrizantis, insinuantes, statuimus annua frequentatione solemniter celebrare, utpote quem specialiter nobis cum beato Gregorio et Augustino et patronum quaerimus et habere indubitanter credimus coram Christo Domino, quem in vita sua semper amavit, et in morte, ut ipsius meruit gratia, magnifice clarificavit. Praeterea quippe, ut praediximus, vestrae sollicitae speculationis curam, et quasi taedio absentati patrisfamilias, ut ita dicam, quodammodo confectam, necnon et generalitatem subjectorum vobis servorum Dei, paternis affatibus fraternisque solatiis, relevare et consolari, ubicunque et in quocunque negotio praevalemus, fatemur nos semper esse paratos. Unde in primis ad confirmationem dilectionis quam erga vos habent penetralia cordis nostri, sermone affectuque apostoli utamur, et cum apostolo simul dicamus: Gratia vobis et pax.

Gratias agimus Deo semper pro omnibus vobis, memoriam facientes in orationibus nostris sine intermissione, memores operis fidei vestrae, et laboris, et charitatis, et sustinentiae spei Domini nostri Jesu Christi, ante Deum et Patrem nostrum. Quod enim jam olim, vivente venerandae memoriae Bonifacio, per scripta nonnulla, et per fideles internuntios, aeque conditum esse constat, idipsum semper revocare ad invicem satis necessarium ducimus, hoc est, ut mutuae pro nobis nostrisque et hic viventibus et hinc obedientibus interpellationes, orationes, missarumque remedia, ad viventem Deum et judicem omnium suppliciter agantur, juxta apostolica monita: Orate, inquit, pro invicem, ut salvemini, et reliqua. Hoc enim modo nobis divinam clementiam complacare dignoscimur, offerentes ei orationum pura libamina. Sic nobis eamdem prosperantem inveniemus in adversis. Etenim ubi Domini, juxta ipsius promissa, praesto est adjutorium, cuncta fugatur malignorum adversitas. Ipse enim dixit: Si duo ex vobis consenserint super terram de omni re quamcunque petierint, fiet illis a Patre meo, qui in coelis est. Hoc enim sagaci solertia studiosius ideo agendum esse judicamus, quia, juxta apostolica praesagia, instant nunc tempora periculosa, et reliqua, quae ipse in eadem prosequitur Epistola. Et quia non est opus scribere vobis de exterioribus calamitatum incursibus, quas frequenter, ut reor, passi estis, id est, persecutionibus, rapinis, odiis, et scandalis, et his similibus. Caeterum, ecce quamplurimis in locis Christianae religionis valide status vacillat, dum pene undique exterius interiusve rerum ecclesiasticarum perturbatur ordo, novellarumque conversationum pravae ubique pene succrescunt sectae; nec mirum, (0830C)dum, post videlicet positis antiquorum Patrum decretis, ac legibus ecclesiasticis relictis, multi juxta proprias adinventiones, prava et plurimorum nociva saluti sentiunt, affirmant, atque agunt, ut scilicet transacto anno a quodam magnae auctoritatis viro dictum et gestum esse constat. Ad haec autem nos, ut timeo, pusillanimes, et minus zelo justitiae accensi, quid aliud in primis agere debemus, quam ut indesinenter suffragia sanctorum postulemus apostolorum, martyrumque Christi, ac venerabilium antistitum Ecclesiarum Dei, ut in hoc, quod vocati et constituti sumus, continuis excubiis, Christi gratia nos faciat perseverare, et ut non simus reprobi, sed magis accepti, non desides, sed solertes, non dispergentes, sed congregantes quoscunque valeamus ad unanimitatem Christianae religionis, et unitatem ecclesiasticae conversationis, quatenus ministerium nostrae dispensationis et laboris solertia ad laudem et gloriam Dei omnipotentis proficiat, ut cum bene servientibus ac placentibus Deo quandoque mereamur audire: Beatus servus quem, cum venerit Dominus, invenerit vigilantem! Amen dico vobis quod super omnia bona sua constituet eum; et ad haec, frequentius ad memoriam, exempli causa, revocemus recordandae memoriae egregius magister et martyr beatus Bonifacius quomodo vel quanta solertia laborarit in doctrina Christi, quanta pericula atque difficultates pro amore Christi et animarum lucro, etiam usque ad ipsam mortem, libenter tolerarit. Et quia Omnipotentis modo familiaris factus est, prudentia vestra solerter attendat, si ejus vos oporteat sacris admonitionibus consentire, et pietatis illius exempla pro viribus sequi. Ille enim quantum illius domesticus factus est quem amavit ante omnia, tantum majora apud eum poterit obtinere. Unde quippe si aliqui subjectorum illius, quibus eum quondam divina dispensatio magisterii loco profecit, ab ejus documentis spiritualibus dissentiunt, vel prava conversatione recedunt, qui defensor illorum in aeterno judicio esse potuit, sit potius accusator, et rationes ab eis cum ipso judice districtius requirit. At vero, e diverso, quicunque illius sacrae institutionis ac doctrinae normulam rite consequuntur, pro certo se sciant, et ipsius Romanae atque apostolicae Ecclesiae, a qua legatus eis et doctor directus est, ac deinde, pariter cum ea, omnium nostrum habere et viventes et morientes in oratione et missarum celebratione, ut supra diximus, perpetuam communionem, si tamen usque ad finem firmam vobis dehinc doctoribus et rectoribus suae salutis, humiliter atque amabiliter, pro Deo et aeterna mercede, non dedignantur obedire, non deficientes aliquando, ut indevoti vel subdoli, sed semper ut bonae indolis discipuli proficientes, et fideliter adhaerentes suae militiae in Christo magistris, ad palmam supernae vocationis Dei et gloriam regni coelestis. Haec salutatoria vestrae sanctitati scripsimus verba, non quasi ignaris aut indigentibus nostrae rusticitatis normula, sed charitatis atque communitionis [communionis] mutuae gratia, contestantes et obsecrantes per omnipotentem Deum et Filium ejus Jesum Christum, et adventum ipsius, et regnum ejus, ut vos, o charissimi, cuncti generaliter cum subjectis vobis in Christo per omnia sitis semper ad invicem fideles adjutores, et unanimes cooperatores, contra omnes orthodoxae fidei inimicos atque haereticos et schismaticos, ac nequissimae conversationis homines. Per hoc enim eritis bonis hominibus amabiles seu laudabiles, et Deo omnipotenti acceptabiles atque chari; et ita, cum ipso praefato beato Patre, et praedecessore vestro, felicem in futuro vocem a judice cunctorum Christo singuli mereatis audire: Euge, inquiet, serve bone et fidelis, quia super pauca fuisti fidelis, supra multa te constituam; intra in gaudium Domini tui. Amen.

Omnipotens Deus vos omnes diu incolumes in suo sancto amore et timore custodire dignetur.

Dilectiss. FF. ac filiis, Cuthberchtus archiepiscop., Lullo coepisc.

EPISTOLA XIII. CYNEHARDUS LULLO. (Anno Domini 756.)

Domino dignissimo, venerando, et merito insigni ac praestantissimo, longe lateque pro Christianae religionis praedicanda doctrina diffamato, et pro conversatione vitae probatissimae celeberrimo, nobis quoque non immerito, ob cognationis nostrae semper memorandae necessitudinem, charissimo, Lullae episcopo, Cineheardus indignus, ut vereor, episcopus Wentanae civitatis, ex intima visceralium medullarum affectione, aeternaliter in Christo salutem.

Perlectis litterarum a tua sanctitate directarum dulcissimis ac nimium placabilibus periodis, in quibus amicabiliter nostram parvitatem comperimus salutatam admonitamque, ut eamdem unitatis observantiam custodiret, quam antecessores nostri fideliter fine tenus observarunt, Dominus Bonifacius archiepiscopus, Christique confessor beatificandus, et Daniel doctissimus Dei plebis famulus, simul et successor ejus Hunfrithus episcoporum mitissimus, etc., quae te melius recoluisse credimus, in caraxatis commendata, mentis diligentissima indagine didicisse curavimus, et gratiarum actiones condignas in quantum sufficimus persolvendo gerimus, quod nostri memoriam, interpositis tantarum spatiis terrarum, marisque magni interluente latitudine, facere dignemini. Et hoc profitemur, quod omnia quae, tua sanctitate suggerente, mandata sunt, studiosissime, Domino favente, complere satagimus, non tantum in spirituali orationum solatio exhibendo, et missarum solemnitate celebranda pro vobis, et pro illis qui in vestris regionibus in Christi consessione obeunt, sed etiam si qua saecularis substantiae solatia vestris usibus profutura in his regionibus adipisci poterimus, vestrae participationi parata erunt. Et hoc petimus, si qua apud vos solamina nobis necessaria, vel ignota, spiritualis quidem scientiae, sive in libris antiquis, qui a nobis non habentur, sive in aliis ecclesiasticis administrationibus, ut nobis libenter participare non negetis. Necnon et si quos saecularis scientiae libros nobis ignotos adepturi sitis, ut sunt de medicinalibus, quorum copia est aliqua apud nos, sed tamen segmenta ultra marina, quae in eis scripta comperimus, ignota nobis sunt et difficilia ad adipiscendum; vel si qua in aliis quibuslibet negotiis, vel speciebus nobis necessariis providetis, communicare dignemini, ut fecistis villosam mittendo. Nomina quoque presbyterorum vestrorum diaconorumque, ac monachorum, vel monacharum, sive caeterorum, quae misistis, per monasteria et per ecclesias nostrae dioecesis direximus ad celebranda pro eis missarum solemnia, et orationum suffragia. Id ipsum facere vestram sanctitatem suppliciter exoramus pro eis, quorum nomina vobis habemus dirigenda, et nominatim cum personis suis scribenda, eorum scilicet qui mihi proprie atque huic Ecclesiae, cui servio, amicissimi, vel subditi fiebant, vel praelati. De nostro quoque vili vestitu parva haec xeniola direximus tuo cultui, quanquam indigna, tamen petimus, accommoda, hoc est, tunica lanea, aliaque linea, sicut mos est apud nos habendi, caligas et peripsemata, orarium, et coculam, et gunnam brevem nostro more consutam, ad indicium plenissimae dilectionis nostrae. Quae te suscipere pro tua humilitate obnixe precamur, habereque ad memoriam mei nominis, saltem aliquod spatium temporis. Caeterum si qua sunt tuae sanctitati insinuanda, portitor hujus epistiunculae viva voce valet enarrare.

Opto te, o charissime frater, orantem pro me orante pro te, in Domino bene valere, felicemque aevo longiore victurum, ad coronam coelestis gloriae postea perventurum, Domine insignis, et Pater praestantissime. Amen.

EPISTOLA XIV. EARDULFUS LULLO. (Circa annum Domini 756.)

Reverendissimo nobisque omnium episcoporum charissimo Lullo coepiscopo Aeardulfus Hrofensis ecclesiae antistes, cum sanctae ecclesiae filio Aeardvulfo rege Cantiae, sinceram in Christi nomine salutem.

Veracium igitur sociorum inter alia amicabilis memorialisque mos esse dignoscitur, cum sese, ob interjacentium terrarum spatia, seu provinciarum exterarum regiones, praesentialiter nequeunt invisere ac salutare, certe per suos fideles nuntios, sive etiam per litteras ad invicem salutationis dirigere verba, et de rebus dignis atque utilibus tractare, ne mens, scilicet, sollicita quid de statu amici divina dispensatione et judicio agatur, vel taedio diutius afficiatur, vel anxia rerum incertitudine quotidie gemat. Quocirca in primis diligentius salutantes, per hunc gerulum, visitantes eminentiam vestram, desiderium quippe habentes audire et nosse eamdem gloriosissimum prosperumque per omnia profectum habere, hoc modis omnibus optantes, ut nos ipsos nostrosque charissimos vestrae beatitudini subnixis commendemus precibus, ut in vestris sacris ac Deo placitis orationibus, et suffragio vestrae paternae pietatis undique, auxiliante Deo, muniti, atque muro protectionis vestrae circumdati, contra omnes infestationes inimici in hac vita, quae tota tentatio est, defensi, et ad illam quae morte vacans et fine carens, vestris almis intercessionibus, pervenire mereamur. Misimus vobis parva xenia, id est reptem ruptilem unam, deprecantes obnixe ut amorem mittentis magis quam censum perpendatis, ob spem meliorum, quod celerius fit orantibus vobis, si

Dominus vitam et vires concesserit. Memores enim sumus verborum omnium quae ex abundantia cordis vestri prolata nostris auribus sonuerunt adimplenda, quae quantum ames amantes te ex omni parte declarabant. Quid enim aliud nobis agendum est, nisi ut charitatem quoad, Deo disponente et finem cunctorum considerante, omnes advixerimus, fideliter ad invicem custodiamus. Praeterea nihilominus et deinceps dum aliquis e nobis alterius vitae vias, ut opto, felices prior ingrediatur, en superveniens sine mora, missis et eleemosynis, itiner illius hinc et inde quantum valeat tueri ac prosperum facere saepius reminiscat ac studeat, obsecrantes obnixe, ut per hunc fratrem nostrum fidelissimum presbyterum, nomine Laearoredum, scripta pietatis tuae ad nos dirigere digneris, quatenus per haec earum quae tibi placita sunt rerum cognitio clarescat, quia habetis sine dubio in eodem praefato presbytero veridicum fidelemque inter nos legatarium; et ideo per illum valebis quaecunque, vivae vocis attestatione, nobis patefacere. Praecedentium quoque nomina propinquorum nostrorum, id est, Irmigi, Noththry, atque Dulichae, omnes Deo dicatae virgines, tibi direximus, postulantes ut in oblationibus missarum et orationum suffragiis habeatis, quia similia nobis ad invicem beneficii rependere parati sumus.

Deus te incolumem custodiat, et in ejus ministerio pollentem longa per temporum spatia custodire dignetur.

Aeardulfus episc. Lullo coepisc.

EPISTOLA XV. MILREDUS LULLO. (Circa annum Domini 756.)

Domino amantissimo et in Christo charissimo Lullae episcopo Milret servus Deo servientium.

Postquam a tua praesentia et a conspectu corporali sanctissimi praesulis et beatissimi patris Bonifacii, nolens, volens, tristis abscedebam, et per varios casus, et multa discrimina rerum, vestris almis orationibus, ad terram nostrae pervenimus nativitatis. Ibi nec dum integro expleto anni circuli curriculo, nuntium ad nos perlatum est triste, beatissimum Patrem de ergastulo carnis ad superna migrasse; si tamen id triste dicere fas est, cum talem ad coeli patronum meruimus praemittere regna, cujus nos sacris intercessionibus, Deo auxiliante, ubique esse suffultos certa credulitate confidimus. Et quamvis praesentis vitae amissum solatium multis et amaris luximus lacrymis, tamen ille qui, suo sanguine fuso, Christo consecratus est martyr, decus et columen omnium quos praesens protulit patria, suo beatissimo agone, optimo labore consummato, gloriosissimo fine peracto, nostra valde moesta majore laetitia mitigat et demulcet pectora. Nos nostram dolemus vicem in valle lacrymarum, et in hac vita, quae tota tentationum plena est, manentes; ille, peregrino labore magno cum sudore expleto, ad gloriosissimam Christi martyr pervenit mortem, et pro nostris, ut credo, excessibus, si Domini sinit pietas, fidelis intercessor in coelesti Jerusalem, cum Christo, beatissima sorte, sanctis conjunctus civibus, superna laetus consistit in arce. Haec de amantissimo Patre, cujus venerabilem vitam et gloriosum finem, ut mihi in notitiam venire facias, totis viribus exopto. Aliud ex sodali collegio dicere menti occurrit, tuamque dulcissimam charitatem intimis obsecro praecordiis, et tanquam tuis pedibus praesentialiter prostratus humiliter imploro, ut fraternam dilectionem, quam inter nos communis Pater beatae recordationis et sanctae memoriae Bonifacius, Christi annuente charitate, sacris conciliavit verbis, almis univit oraculis, non transitoria, sed fixa recordatione tua recondas in corde, quia mihi et tibi valde profuturum, omni ambiguitate postposita, scio, si tam egregii doctoris praecepta implere conamur, meque omnium fratrum tuorum minimum in meritis, fraterna charitate instruere, sacris munire praeceptis, almis orationibus fulcire, o amantissime praesul, non pigeat, unde fateor et fida promissione spondeo, vestris sincerissimis jussionibus, juxta qualitatem virium, in omnibus libenter me esse secuturum, et firma dilectione fidam amicitiam, quandiu spiritus hos regit artus, vitalisque status his moribundis inhabitat membris, tecum servare intima charitate, Deo teste, profiteor, et totis viribus medullitus admodum exopto, ut fiat, Christo tribuente, quod scriptum est: Erant illis omnia communia. Sed haec omnia, quae breviter a nobis dicta sunt, si Deus omnipotens prosperum concedit iter, per gerulos istarum litterarum plenius et verbaliter tibi indicare curavi. Misimus praeterea parva munuscula, quae optamus, ut ea dilectione accipiatis, qua a nobis, Deo teste, destinata sunt.

Vestram dilectionem pro nostris excessibus intercedentem Christus tueri dignetur.

Librum Pyrpyri metri ideo non misi, quia Guthbertus episc. adhuc reddere distulit. Immanuel. Epistola Milredi episc. offerenda Lullae episc.

EPISTOLA XVI. TRECEA LULLO. (Circa annum Domini 756.)

Domino in Domino venerabiliter diligendo et delectabiliter honorando Lullo, episcopatus infula fungenti, Trecea supplex vernaculus in Christo perennem salutem.

Tempore nuper transacto, vestrae almitatis litteraturam usque ad nostrae mediocritatis praesentiam fido gestante gerulo delatam, exsultantibus pectorum praecordiis, et laetis oculorum orbibus contemplantes satis libenter suscipimus, et maxime in vestra sancta promissione, quam ordo apicum vestrorum innotuit, ut vestris assiduis ac sacris orationibus nostram fragilitatem defendere vellet; ita et nostra imperfecta mediocritas undique pene in omnibus bonis vestram beatitudinem orationibus intimis, Deo ubique auxiliante, deprecando poscere Deum prompta est, necnon et dilectionem fraternitatis erga vestram clementiam observare, secundum vires, velle demonstramus, Domino nostro Jesu Christo docente ac dicente: Hoc est praeceptum meum, ut diligatis invicem. Et item: In hoc cognoscent omnes quia mei estis discipuli, si dilectionem habueritis ad invicem, etc. Item de eadem beatus Petrus primus et princeps apostolorum sententiam promulgavit, dicens: Estote itaque prudentes, et vigilate in orationibus, ante omnia mutuam in vobismetipsis charitatem continuam habentes, quia charitas cooperit multitudinem peccatorum, etc. Nostra ergo, ni fallor, parvitas non utcunque vestris est roborata oppido patrociniis. Idcirco audaciter rogare praesumimus vestram beatam ac vere benedictam almitatem, ut nostram, viventes in hac lacrymarum valle, tum etiam in gloriosissima praescientia Dei in Christo pausantes, assiduis ac sacris orationibus vestrarum studiis Domino Deo commendare dignemini. Ego quoque minimus Ecclesiae servus supplici per Dominum deprecatione rogito, ut me cum mea familia, Domino Deo cuncta dispensante ac rite regente, inter caeteros fideles vestros amicos in commune benigne suscipiatis, qui proprio dicor nomine Aldbertus, diaconatus officio fungens, licet indignus, ut, sancti gradus ministerium olim acceptum vestris saluberrimis intercessionibus meliorando, de die in diem proficiam. Almitatem vestram pro nobis orantem summus arbiter orbis ab alta coelorum arce tueri dignetur. Valete in Domino.

EPISTOLA XVII. BOTWINUS LULLO. (Circa annum Domini 756.)

Venerandae dignitatis Lullo episc. Botwinus abb. optabilem in Christo salutem.

Litterae auctoritatis tuae, quas cum divinae pietatis studio usque ad nos direxisti, laetificaverunt me valde, quia tu, imbre coelestis roris illectus, ultimum me servunculum servorum Dei cum tam magna fide divini amoris, saeculariaeque dignitatis munere visitare dignatus fuisti. Gratias ago Deo, petens, cum intimae charitatis desiderio, ut fidus fautor mihi per celsitudinem sanctitatis tuae coram Christo Jesu existas, in istoque saeculo serena mente amicus, si rector rerum omnium istius vitae in itinere me longius super te sudare dijudicat, ploro indesinenter precans, cum omni caterva quae Christo Domino sub mea conditione deservit, divinae misericordiae solatia animae tuae largiri, ut tu simili modo ecclesiarum tuarum subsidia mihi praestare digneris. Haec quoque modica munuscula, id est, III lacernas almitati tuae mitto optans ut accepta sint.

EPISTOLA XVIII. WICBERTUS LULLO. (Circa annum Domini 756.)

Sanctissimo et a Deo semper conservato Domino Lullo episcopo Wicbertus, servus servorum Dei, quanquam indignus, abbas, et vester in omnibus (Deus scit) bene cupiens et fidelis in vinculo charitatis colligatus.

Suscepta vestra alimonia, sancta cuncta congregatio monachorum nostrorum pro vobis singulos psalterios Domino decantaverunt, et sacerdotes quinas missas fecerunt per singulos, ut vobis Dominus pristinam sanitatem tribueret, et dixi ad illos, vestra voluntate, quomodo nobis mandastis ut hic pro tempore devenire jubebatis. Sed omnes consona una concordia responderunt, quod nostra voluntas in omnibus est, ipsius infirmitati compatescere, et sicut proprium fratrem, ita circa illum omni charitate impendere. Sed vos modo si vultis, sic venire potestis, quomodo in vestra propria casa, et nos in omnibus, in quantum possumus, charitate pristina exigentes vestrae volumus compatescere infirmitati. In orationibus tuis commendamus nos, sanctissime Pater.

Sanctissimo Domino Lullo episcopo. Wicbertus indignus abbas.

EPISTOLA XIX. DOTO LULLO. (Circa annum Domini 756.)

Domino sancto sanctorum, quia meritis coaequando, et a nobis cum summa veneratione diligendo, in Christo Patre Lullo, coepiscopo, Doto servus servorum Dei, etiam et omnes monachi sancti Petri apostolorum principis degentes sub norma sanctae regulae, aeternam in Domino nostro Jesu Christo ad sanctitatem vestram destinare curavimus salutem

Ideo omnipotenti Domino gratias referimus, ut omnia quae circa vos sunt prospera non solum habemus, sed et hoc indesinenter sedulis precibus Domini misericordiam imploramus, ut vitam vestram longaevis faciat hic gaudere temporibus, et illic in aeterna beatitudine cum sanctis suis faciat pariter exsultare triumphis. De caetero quamvis, amantissime Pater, terrarum longitudine separati videmur, tamen et terrarum longinquitas non dividit mente, quos charitas divina conjunxit in corde. Idcirco comperiat sanctitas vestra quia nos omnes per obedientiam almi Patris nostri Dodoni abbatis, et pro amore vestro et omni sollicitudine pro vobis, et devotissima sancta congregatione vestra, a Deo vobis commissa, in nostris assiduis precibus Domini misericordiam exorare non desinemus. Igitur cum salutationis officiis, humili prece deposcimus, ut istam familiam Christi et sancti Petri in vestra commemoratione semper habeatis, et ipsi pro omnibus amicis vestris tam episcopis et eorum clero, quam abbatibus et eorum monachis, seu et abbatissis vel Deo dicatis in ista congregatione sancti Petri, oratores vestros tam vivos quam defunctos in vestra mercede commemorare faciatis, ut in sacris orationibus illorum eam assidue memorare debeant, quatenus per illorum suffragia olim optatam adire mereamur patriam paradisi. Similiter vos deprecamur, ut omnium amicorum vestrorum nomina tam vivorum, quam defunctorum, per praesentem fratrem nostrum Saganaldum, per breve ad nos dirigere faciatis, ut ipsos, sicut de aliis fratribus nostris facimus, ita in nostris assiduis orationibus ipsos memorare debeamus. Gratia regis coelestis custodiat vos semper. Amen.

Indiculus directus ad Lullonum episcopum. Emmanuel nobiscum sit.

EPISTOLA XX. CYNEARDUS LULLO. (Circa annum Domini 756.)

Domino magnopere diligendo, et nobis omnium peregrinantium pro Christi amore charissimo, Lullo antistiti, Cineardus indignus, ut vereor, episcopus in Christo salutem

Libenter ergo suscipimus fratrem a te ad nos usque directum cum dulcedine donorum vestrorum et gratias agentes Deo et vobis, quod nostri memoriam ex tam remotis terrarum finibus facere dignemini. Et ideo sicut vos velle comperimus memores sumus vestri, in quantum, Domino adjuvante, permittimur semper in orationibus nostris, obsecrantes, ut quod fideli, ac firmissimo coepistis animo usque ad finem firmum retineatis; quanquam multis tribulationibus tundimini, quas propemodum omnes sancti soliti sunt a saeculo perpeti, nec tamen Christo cooperante, et confirmante illorum constantiam, deficiebant. Modici munusculi quantulamcunque parvitatem charitatis tantummodo intuitu direximus, hoc est, de nostro vestitu indumentum, sicut solent prodecessores nostri prodecessoribus tuis destinare, quod te pro humilitate et mansuetudine tua suscipere dignanter, et uti suppliciter precamur.

Valere te in Christo, et ut vere felicem semper optamus.

EPISTOLA XXI. [...] LULLO. (Circa annum Domini 756).

Sanctissimo atque venerabili episcopo Lullo servus servorum Dei visceralem in Domino salutem.

Rogo te, o dilectissime frater, sicut optime in te credo, ut non immemor sis, sed semper sagacissima mente ad memoriam reducas antiquam amicitiam nostram, quam inter nos habuimus in Maldubia civitate, quando Eaba abbas in amabili charitate nutrivit, et hoc signum recordor, quod pro nomine vocavit te Irtel, idcirco salutat te Hereca abbas in salutatione sancta, et omnis congregatio quae in sua coenobiali vita manet, quia dignos nos in memoriam habuisti tecum. Qui autem perseveraverit in pace usque in finem, hic salvus erit. Vale, amabilis, feliciter in aevum; meus dilectus, Deo electus, quia charitas pretium non habet.

Hoc signum Hereca abbatem fecit.

EPISTOLA XXII. CUTHBERTUS LULLO. (Circa annum Domini 758.)

Desiderantissimo et suavissimo in Christi dilectione amico Lullo episcopo, et omnium antistitum charissimo, Cuthbertus discipulus Bedae presbyteri salutem.

Gratanter quidem munuscula tuae charitatis suscepi, et eo gratantius, quo te haec intimo devotionis affectu mittere cognovi, id est, holosericam ad reliquias beatae memoriae Beda magistri nostri, ob recordationem et illius venerationem destinasti. Et rectum quidem mihi videtur ut tota gens Anglorum in omnibus provinciis, ubicunque reperti sunt, gratias Deo referant, quia tam mirabilem virum, praeditum diversis donis, tamque ad exercenda dona studiosum, similiterque in bonis moribus viventem, Deus illis in sua natione donavit, quia per experimentum, ad pedes ejus nutritus, hoc quod narro didici. Similiterque mihimet ipsi coopertorium variatum ad tegendum scilicet, propter frigus, meum corpus misisti, quod videlicet omnipotenti Deo et beato Paulo apostolo ad induendum altare, quod in ejus ecclesia Deo consecratum est, cum magno gaudio dedi, quia et ego sub ejus protectione in hoc monasterio XL et III annos vixi. Nunc vero, quia rogasti aliquid de opusculis beati Patris, cum meis pueris, juxta vires, quod potui tuae dilectioni praeparavi: libellos de Viro Dei Cudbercto, metro et prosa compositos, tuae voluntati direxi; et si plus potuissem, libenter voluissem, quia praesentia praeteritae hiemis multum horribiliter insulam nostrae gentis in frigore, et gelu, et ventorum, et imbrium procellis, diu lateque depressit, ideoque scriptoris manus, ne in plurimorum librorum numerum perveniret, retardata est; sed et ante sex annos per Hunwini meum presbyterum illuc ad vestra loca advenientem, et Romam videre desiderantem, aliqua parva xenia, cultellos videlicet XX et gunnam de pellibus lutrarum factam tuae fraternitati misi. Ille quoque presbyter Hunwini, ad urbem quae vocatur Beneventum perveniens, ibi de hac luce migravit. Quapropter neque per illum, neque per tuorum aliquem, utrum ista ad te pervenerint, ulla responsio unquam mihi reddita est. Duo vero pallia subtilissimi operis, unum albi, alterum tincti coloris cum libellis, et clocam, qualem ad manum habui, tuae paternitati mittere curavimus, precorque ut meam petitionem et necessitatem non spernas. Si aliquis homo in tua sit parochia qui vitrea vasa bene possit facere, cum tempus arrideat, mihi mittere digneris, aut si fortasse ultra fines est in potestate cujusdam alterius, sine tua parochia, rogo ut fraternitas tua illi suadeat ut ad nos usque perveniat, quia ejusdem artis ignari et inopes sumus, et si hoc fortasse contingit ut aliquis de vitrifactoribus cum tua diligentia, Deo volente, ad nos usque venire permittatur, cum benigna mansuetudine, vita comite, illum suscipio. Delectat me quoque cytharistam habere, qui possit citharisare in cithara, quam nos appellamus rottae, quia citharam habeo, et artificem non habeo. Si grave non sit, et istum quoque meae dispositioni mitte. Obsecro ut hanc meam rogationem ne despicias, et risioni non deputes. De opusculis vero beatae recordationis Beda, quae adhuc descripta non habes, promitto, (0839D)me, si vixerimus, tuae voluntati adjuvaturum.

Abbas Cuthbertus te te bis terque salutat;

Te Deus omnipotens salvum conservet in aevum.

EPISTOLA XXIII. EANVULT LULLO. (Anno Domini 758.)

Domino desiderabili ac jure venerabili episcopo Lullo, Eanvult servus Christi Jesu, una cum conservis qui mecum his in locis suavissimum Evangelii jugum, pro invenienda in coelis requie, trahere gaudent, perpetem in Domino salutem.

Multo quidem gaudio delectatum est cor nostrum, magna exsultatione lingua insonuit, dum tantae vir eruditionis ac sanctitatis ad nos litteras transmiserat. Quapropter paternam tuae charitatis reverentiam obsecramus, ut, semper nostri memor, supplices pro nobis domino preces offerre non refrageris. Nos tui quoque scias semper existere memores, si quid tam vilium apud dominum valet deprecatio servorum. Quantum enim de omni vestro profectu gavisi sumus, quantamque super his quae in peregrinis locis vobis prospera cesserunt laetitiam haberemus [...] Teque nosse volumus, quod hoc perpetualiter studium charitatis tuis meritis impetrantibus observemus, tuamque per omnia desideremus amicitiam mereri, volentes ipsi per omnia tuae justae voluntatis obtemperare decretis, etiam Domino procurante, quando, ingrediente te viam universae (0840B)terrae, atque ad praemia vitae aeternae perducto, tunc tuum venerabile nomen disponimus scribere cum nominibus episcoporum nostrorum, et cum nominibus omnium praecedentium fratrum hujus monasterii.

Orantem pro nobis almam paternitatis vestrae coronam coelestis gratia custodiat, dilectissime in Christo antistes [...] Scripta indict. 11, IX Kal. Junias [...] ad Jul. epist. epis.

EPISTOLA XXIV. MAGINGOOZ LULLO. (Circa annum Domini 760.)

Venerando sacerdoti Christi, amore prorsus ac reverentia pariter a nobis studio peculiari contuendo, Lullo episcopo Magingooz servus servorum Dei perennem in Christo salutem.

In colloquio nuper venerandae fraternitatis tuae comperti sumus quia consilium proximi nostri cujusdam minus caute, saeculi impedimento postposito, viam religionis ingredi cupientis prudentia vestra praevenire utiliore consulto voluisset, qui, ut arbitror, his verbis velut nomine proprio designatur. Et revera visum mihi est non posse aliter compleri circa illum officium debitae felicitatis et charitatis, nisi cum pluribus de eadem re necessario sollicitis contendatur, ne hunc fortasse in ipso itinere, quo desiderium ducit, incauta praesumptio supplantet, sed necessarium existimo ut diligentius provideatur quo pacto vel quibus instrumentis peregrinationis illius, quam sicut scitis optimam [...] stabilitas et possibilis, et si fieri potuerit, inexcusabilis, iis cum quibus praesens causa agenda est, omni rationis firmitate comprobetur. Quapropter nostrae parvitati indicare per litteras non gravemini utrum vobis videatur an communi sermone unius epistolae exhortatio mittatur, an uterque nostrum a se epistolam mittat; quod si profuturum judicetis ut commune et unum a nobis indiculum dirigatur, a vestra charitatis industria rogo ut conficiatur. Si non fieri posse putaveritis, ut sine aliqua praesenti, sive nostra, sive caeterorum servorum Dei, collatione consulto decenti et integra soliditatis valeat perpetrari. Quid itaque vobis profuturum videatur, ut a nobis hac de re agatur per litteras, hujus epistiunculae portitori traditas, nobis indicare dignemini.

Valere bonitatem vestram, et in Christo proficere pro nobis intercedentem, integris desideriis optamus. Off. Lullo episc.

EPISTOLA XXV. CUTHBERTUS LULLO. (Circa annum Domini 760.)

Domino in Domino dilectissimo et fidelissimo amico Lullo episcopo Cuthbertus abbas salutem.

Multum gratanter accepi litteras sive etiam munera, hoc est, villosam et sindonem, quae tua fraternitas ad me mittere dignata est; et eo gratantius, quod ex intima charitate ea destinata esse non ambigo. Unde recompensationem beneficii istius reddens et ipse tui quotidianis in precibus curam habere non cesso; simul etiam nomina fratrum quae ad nos misisti cum nominibus hujus monasterii fratrum dormientium in Christo scripta continentur, ita ut pro illis nonaginta et eo amplius missas facere praeceperim. Insuper etiam librum, quem clarissimus Ecclesiae Dei magister Beda de Aedificio templi composuit, ad consolationem tuae peregrinationis mittere curavi, tuam fraternitatem humiliter obsecrans, ut olim condictae inter nos amicitiae foedera usque ad finem firmum custodire digneris, in hoc videlicet maxime, quod cum tuis omnibus, quos tibi divina dispensatio voluit esse subjectos, pro infirmitatibus meis apud supernum Judicem sedulus intercessor existas. Lullo episc.

Dominus omnipotens fraternitatem tuam in suo semper amore conservet.

EPISTOLA XXVI. CENE LULLO. (Circa annum Domini 760.)

Domino beatissimo omnique honore nominando Lullae episcopo Coena, servus servorum Dei, perpetuae gratiae salutem.

Acceptis tuae beatitudinis, Pater excellentissime, litteris, multa sum laetitia delibutus, ita ut totis praecordiorum intestinis gaudens lacrymaverim, beatum mihi ac profuturum aestimans tanti Patris perfrui amicitia, ideoque omni cordis aviditate tuam desiderabilem amplector pietatem, tua inhianter condelector charitate, ea potissimum causa, quia salutaria dilectionis praecepta divinitatis, indita nobis rememorans, nec non et aliquandiu fautorem sive consiliarium adoptans laboribus nostrae parvitatis, quem misericors omnium bonorum largitor nobis, in te sua benigna providentia, ut credimus, praeordinavit. Quapropter, dulcissime frater, in quascunque sanctae pacis ditiones vocabis, lubens, festinus gaudensque totus, pleno corde advenio. Insuper plurimis obsecrationem lacrymis deprecor, ut nostri quantulamcunque in tuis sanctis orationibus habere memoriam digneris, semperque bene coeptae pietatis promissa custodias, quia perseveranti gloriosa retributionis impenditur corona, mercesque futurae felicitatis in fine cujusque operis spectatur. Illud vero quod de libris inquisisti marinis aestibus terram advectantibus, omnino incognitum est. Caeterum libri cosmographicorum necdum nobis ad manum venerunt; nec alia apud nos exemplaria, nisi picturis et litteris permolesta. Jam saepius mihimet perscribere destinavi, sed nondum potui scriptores acquirere. Forte tuis adjutus supplicationibus [...]

Sanctitatem vestram ad protectionem electae Dominae rex salvator conservet in aevum.

Scio, Pater, quod illa, quae charitatis gratia misi, a te visa non sunt. Vivendo felix Christi laurate triumphis, Vita tuis, saeclo specimen, charissime coelo, Justitiae cultor, verus pietatis amator, Defendens vigili sanctas tutamine mandras, Pascua florigeris pandens praedulcia campis, Judice centenos portans veniente maniplos.

Offerenda Lullo Episcopo viro clarissimo.

EPISTOLA XXVII. WIGBERTUS LULLO. (Circa annum Domini 760.)

Domino vere beato, atque omni officio charitatis venerando, Lullae, gratia Dei episcopo, Wigbertus presbyter vester fidelis servus, optabilem in Christo salutem.

Vestris orationibus meritisque suffragantibus, ut credimus, et pro certo scimus prospera nobis terrae marisque itinera, postquam a vobis ieramus, Dei clementia concessit, amicosque et propinquos sanos et incolumes invenimus, benigneque suscipientes omnia necessaria tam in possessionibus agrorum, quam in jumentis et pecoribus, aliisque suppellectilibus sponte nobis tribuentes. Quod usque hodie absque ulla contradictione habentes, tuam sanctam fraternitatem, quae nos semper et adjuvare et consolari consueverat, rogamus et obsecramus, ut videas et consideres quid nobis utilius agendum sit. Omnia enim tibi nota sunt; et hoc et illud, quidquid tibi bonum videtur, hoc me fateor laeto animo fecisse, et tuum salubre consilium in nullo sprevisse. Si tibi videtur, ut ad vos pergamus, utiles, ut credimus, viri et, ut aiunt, boni in nostro desiderant esse comitatu. Sin autem aliud magis placet, tamen, cum nostro sermone et consilio, si vobis sic videtur, visitare vos desiderant. De qua re, quid tibi videtur fac sciamus. Sed quid magis moror, cum litterae tuae usque ad nos veniunt, quas, ut isti praesenti portitori litterarum mearum tribuas, obsecramus. Quidquid in illis jusseris, aut suaseris, Deo permittente et vita comite, libenter faciemus. Multum jam vitae nostrae fluctuando et negligendo, quasi extra nos fusi, peregimus, tandem aliquando ut ad nosmetipsos redeamus, necesse est, scientes scriptum quod qui seminat in lacrymis, in gaudio metet, et ideo vitae nostrae quod restat, cum vestro consilio transcurrere curamus. De caetero autem si in regione gentis nostrae, id est Saxonum, aliqua janua divinae misericordiae aperta sit, remandare nobis id ipsum curate quam multi, cum Dei adjutorio, in eorum auxilium festinare cupiunt. Omnia ista, quae longo sermone perstrinximus, tu mente pervigili, quid melius agendo sit, pertracta, et litteris intimare tua sancta almitas non pigeat. Vale.

Ego Hrothuin dudum aliquid vobiscum; nunc autem his positus scribens, legens docensque quod legi, multum vos saluto, obsecrans ut eo animo erga me sitis, quo et ego circa vos sum positus. Saluta omnes qui amant Dominum nostrum Jesum Christum.

EPISTOLA XXVIII. BREGWINUS LULLO. (Circa annum Domini 761.)

Reverendissimo et in Christo charissimo fratri Lullo episcopo Bregwinus, servus servorum Dei, perpetuam in Christi nomine salutem.

Dies multi elapsi sunt ex quo sollicitus praeoptabam ut, Deo favente, tandem aliquando prosperum iter legatarii nostri perveniendi ad beatitudinem vestram invenire potuissent, quia per hos, scilicet proxime decurrentes, priores annos, plurimae ac diversae inquietudines apud nos in Britanniae, vel in Galliae partibus audiebantur existere, et hoc videlicet nostrum desiderabile propositum saepius impedivit, et perterrendo valde prohibuit, de nostris aliquos ad vos dirigere per tam incertas tamque [...] crebris infestationibus improborum hominum in provinciis Anglorum, seu Galliae regiones. Nunc vero pace ac tuitione nobis a principibus indubitanter undique promissa, misimus ad vestram venerabilem fraternitatem hunc praesentem fratrem istarum praesentium litterarum bajulum, Hildeberchtum nomine, reminiscens videlicet qualiter inter nos in civitate Romana de amicitiae conventione colloquium habuimus, quod etiam nos servare omnimodis confitemur. Quapropter et ego nunc, in tuae beatitudinis amicitia confisus, ut secundum quod antecessores nostri inter se facere non cessarunt, ita etiam et nos facere similiter adoptamus, mittentes verba suavissima salutationis et pacis, ut evangelicus sermo impleatur in nobis, quod ejus esse discipuli mereamur, si dilectionem habuerimus ad invicem. Idcirco tibi indicare curavimus nos misisse vestrae beatitudini parva quaedam munuscula, non parva siquidem charitate, id est capsam unam ad officium quidem sacerdotale ex ossibus fabricatam, salutationis tantummodo ac benedictionis causa, per Ishardum religiosum presbyterum, ut ea quae nostra sunt benigne suscipiatis, similiterque et nos a vobis bona recipere optamus. Insuper etiam, omnium fratrum charissime, pro certo hoc nosse tuam amabilem devotionem, Deo teste, desidero, quod tuae sanctitatis dilectionem in eumdem charitatis locum et fraternae societatis consolatium libenter suscipio, atque tenacius contineo, in quo videlicet beati Patris et praedecessoris tui Bonifacii semper inconcussa mansit, et permanet jugiter reposita dilectio, ut inter nos quoque et nostros deinceps familiaris ac spiritualis amicitia, tam ad animarum nostrarum remedia in orationibus et missarum celebrationibus, quam ad hujus vitae quaeque competentia fraternaque suffragia, fideliter persistat. Et ad haec quoque quae praemisi magnopere tua perfici dilectione desidero, ut omnes quippe sacerdotes Dei et familias benedicti ac beati Bonifacii martyris Christi diligenter atque amabiliter ex meo salutes nomine, horterisque pro nobis, quod et pro ipsis facere non desistimus, omnipotentis Dei clementiam obnixis exorare precibus. De redditione vero praefatae rei, sive per verba fratris nostri, sive etiam per litteras tuae fraternae pietatis nos certiorare jubeto.

Omnipotentis Dei pietas sua nos protectione muniat, et ad utilitatem plurimorum sanctitatis vestrae sincerissimam charitatem jugiter in perpetuum conservare et custodire dignetur.

Diem vero depositionis religiosae Christi famulae Buggan celebramus, quae fuit honorabilis abbatissa, cujus etiam dies depositionis fuit VI Kal. Jan. Rogavit me obnixe, dum adhuc viveret, ut hoc vestrae beatitudini transmitterem. Et sicut speravit et credidit, ita facere curate, quoniam illius pater atque patronus fuit in Christo Bonifacius episcopus.

EPISTOLA XXIX. LULLUS CENAE. (Circa annum Domini 762.)

Fratri et consacerdoti et meritis domino charissimo Coena summi pontificatus infula praedito Lullus, exiguus servus servorum Dei, perennem in Christo salutem.

Sanctitatis tuae reverentiam humiliter obsecro, ut amicitiae inter nos olim in Christo copulatae, et semel coeptae, perpes reminisci digneris, ne veterescat, et oblivioni tradatur, quam coram Deo fideli sponsione pepigimus. Pro nomine enim Christi in contumeliis et tribulationibus gloriari et exaltatione Ecclesiae ejus nos oportet, quae quotidie tunditur, premitur atque fatigatur, quia moderni principes novos mores novasque leges secundum sua desideria condunt. Idcirco excellentiam tuam jugem precatricem, pro animae nostrae salute, subnixa prece flagitamus. Assiduis enim corporis aegritudinibus cum mentis anxietate cogor ex hac aerumnosa et periculis plenissima vita exire, redditurus pio et districto judici rationem. Parva vero munuscula dilectioni tuae direxi hoc est, pallam holosericam optimi generis, per gerulum harum litterarum. Obsecro ut quemlibet horum librorum acquiras et nobis mittere digneris, quos beatae memoriae Beda presbyter exposuit, ad consolationem peregrinationis nostrae; id est, in primam partem Samuelis usque ad mortem Saulis, libros quatuor: sive in Esdram et Nehemiam libros tres, vel in Evangelium Marci libros quatuor. Gravia forte postulo, sed nihil grave verae charitati injungo.

EPISTOLA XXX. WIGBERTUS LULLO. (Circa annum Domini 762.)

Domino sancto ac beatissimo, mihique omni affectu semper charissimo Lullae gratia Dei episcopo, Wigbertus exiguus familiae Christi famulus immarcescibilem sempiternae sospitatis salutem.

Magno etenim repletus sum gaudio, valdeque hilarescit animus meus, cognita a nonnullis tua beata sospitate. Quamque, Dei gratia concedente, ut semper habeas, optamus, memoremque nostri esse in tuis sanctis orationibus, Dei gratia concedente, et vestris meritis, ut credimus, suffragantibus, sani et incolumes mare transivimus, nostramque patriam pervenimus, vestraque dona episcopis, abbatibus amicisque vestris, sicut mandastis, obtulimus, et juxta modulum nostri ingenii sermones vestros voluntatemque vestram intimare curavimus. Illi autem fecerunt sicut erant edocti, humiliter, gratanterque omnia suscipientes, magnas gratias Christo Domino referentes, quod vestra sublimitas eorum parvitatem per dona simulque et litteras visitare dignata est, vestramque communionem et familiae vestrae instantiam orationum semper se habituros esse promittentes; nomenque tuum, ut charissimorum suorum, in ecclesiis suis scribentes, memoriamque tui tam viventis quam defuncti jugiter se facturos esse dicentes, epistolasque suas missuros scriptas, ut eis placet, promittentesque omnia quae longis sermonibus protrahimus, iste portitor harum litterarum melius tibi verbis intimare potest, quem vobis presbyterum transmittere curavimus; credentes et confidentes quod utile vas sit in domo Domini, quem ut benigne et honorifice, si dignus sit, vestra sanctitas accipere et habere, quod noster et amicus et propinquus est, dignata sit, obsecramus. Nos igitur, quod celare non possumus, amici et propinqui nostri isto anno a se relinquere nolunt, et ideo nuntios meos ad vos direxi, obsecrans vos humili supplicatione per Domini misericordiam, ut et vota et sermones, quibus me vobis constrinxi, vestra clementia dignata sit absolvere et per epistolam tuam, per nuntios meos revertentes, quid agere debeam insinues. Fateor enim tibi per Deum, quod contra voluntatem tuam nulla dignitas saecli, nulla saecularis amicitia, me hic ullo modo retinere potest, maxime quod te super omnes homines diligo, Deus testis est. Si autem tibi bonum videtur, et tua voluntas sit, ut ad vos citius redeam, Ecclesiae et ministerio, cui ante deservivi, me dimittas, de uno rogo et obsecro. Amici mei, et propinqui, et terram, et haereditatem suam mihi promittunt, et dare disponunt, si hic cum eis permanere dispono; sin autem, alienis permittere debent. Et ideo, mi domine, per prudentiam tuam et cor intelligibile, pertracta et considera quid tibi bonum videtur et rectum, et illud, ut dixi, per litteras intima. Vita etenim comite et Deo concedente, quod jubes facere dispono.

Orantem pro nobis beatitudinem vestram divina misericordia in perpetuum custodire dignetur. Amen.

Ego Hrothuin quondam cognatus tuus, saluto te, multum rogans ut quidquid reprehensibiliter scriptum reperies, indoctae imperitiae ignoscas. Utinam, si fieri potest, et si Dei voluntas sit, ut facie ad faciem videamus nos! Vale et memento nostri.

Macarius polaris aulae pantocrator clemens diu vos incolumes custodire dignetur.

EPISTOLA XXXI. LULLUS CUTHBERTO. (Circa annum Domini 772.)

Sancto ac venerabili in Christo fratri Cuthberto abbati Lullus exiguus servus servorum Dei perennem in Christo salutem.

Charitas quae desinere nescit nunquam veterascit, interni ardorem ignis vix in se sola continere valet. Idcirco placuit nostrae mediocritati de tua sospitate cognoscere, ut tecum in Domino gratularer, ut scires, quae circa fragilitatem meam justo judicio Dei geruntur. Cogor enim continua corporis aegritudine de hac luce fugitiva, et valle lacrymarum, pio et districto Judici rationem redditurus migrare. Idcirco suppliciter obsecro, ut pro animae meae salute enixius Dominum depreceris. Misimus etiam tuae dilectioni parva munuscula, unam pallam holosericam. Petimus etiam ut ad consolationem non solum peregrinationis, sed etiam infirmitatis nostrae, libros istos a beatae memoriae Beda expositos, mittere digneris, de Aedificatione templi, vel in Cantica canticorum, sive epigrammatum heroico metro sive elegiaco compositorum, si fieri potest, omnes; sin autem, de Aedificatione templi libros tres. Fortassis difficilis petitio, sed nihil arbitror esse difficile verae charitati.

Usque ad decrepitam valeas aetatem cum omnibus qui tecum Domino Deo deserviunt.

Nomina quoque fratrum et amicorum nostrorum de hac luce migrantium tuae charitati commendantes, quae sunt [...]

EPISTOLA XXXII. CYNEWULFUS LULLO. (Circa annum Domini 772.)

Domino beatissimo et speciali amore venerando Lullo episcopo ego Cynewulfus, rex occidentalium Saxonum, una cum episcopis meis, nec non cum caterva satraparum, aeternam sospitatis in Domino salutem.

Tibi testificamur quod juxta modum nostrae possibilitatis, quidquid tua sanctitas desideraverit, sive jusserit, libenter agere parati sumus, ut cum reverendissimo et sanctissimo viro Dei praedecessore tuo Bonifacio pepigimus, sive in orationibus Deo devotis, seu in aliis quibuslibet rebus, in quibus humana fragilitas, Deo disponente, mutuis alterutrum solatiis egere comprobatur; te pariter obsecrantes ut pro nostra parvitate, proque pace congregationis nostrae, Domino supplicare cum eis qui tecum invocant nomen Domini Jesu memineris. Istarum vero litterarum portitorem a vobis ante destinatum vestrae almitati committimus, quia fideliter vobis obedire in omnibus curavit.

Omnipotens Deus, qui dispersa congregat, et congregata custodit, ipse vos sua gratia protegat, et vestri laboris fructum in aeterna patria nos videre concedat.

EPISTOLA XXXIII. AMALARDUS ET WIDO LULLO. (Circa annum Domini 774.)

Domino, et Patri Riculfo, archiepiscopo, quem gratia aeterni Regis perpetualiter, ad salutem multorum, et Ecclesiae catholicae defensionem, conservare dignetur, Amalardus et Wido, omnisque congregatio sancti Petri ex monasterio Horbach, in Domino Deo salvatore nostro salutem praesumpsimus mittere.

De caetero notum sit pietati vestrae quia in quantum Deus nos exaudire dignatur, oratores vestri incessanter sumus, et attentius esse cupimus. Comperiat siquidem . . . . magnitudinis vestrae, quia misimus presbyterum nostrum, Macharium nomine, ad nostras ecclesias quae in vestra parochia sitae esse videntur, ut ibidem, solito more, officium perageret. Sed dictum nobis ab eodem presbytero fuit quod auctoritatis vestrae magnitudo juberet non ibidem eum esse officium divinum celebraturum, quia nescimus si aliqua suggestio auribus pietatis vestrae a Bernario episcopo pervenisset, quia idem dominus Bernarius episcopus misit ei unum caballum pascere de nostro stipendio, unde nos vivere debemus, nescimus si pro hac causa factum hoc sit. Nunc deprecamur ut accepta licentia idem presbyter a vobis, liceat ei Domino Jesu Christo et sanctorum eidem in loco reliquiis officium solito more persolvere, ne et domus Dei et reliquiae illius honor sic remaneant sine sacerdote, lumine et officio. Nec nos non habemus illis in partibus sacerdotem qui illud officium ibidem peragere possit, nisi istum. Ideo deprecamur vos ut tale praeceptum et licentia ei a vobis tribuatur, ne tam diu, sicut deprecati sumus, domus Dei et reliquiae illius honor sic, sicut modo, remaneant.

Gratia Domini nostri Jesu Christi vos in praesenti faciat pollere, et in aeterna beatitudine feliciter secum regnare.

Obtineant, obtineant, quaeso, preces nostrae auribus pietatis vestrae, electe Dei, quatenus et aliorum profecta merces vobis magna reddatur a Domino Jesu Christo.

1

LETTER I

LULLUS TO DALHUNO.
Year of Our Lord 752.

 To the most reverend brother Dalhuno, Lullus, unworthy deacon, long ago, serving in the office of the diaconate without the prerogative of merits, wishes you a desirable greeting in the Lord.

 I beseech your clemency with deepest prayers, that you may deign to support the hull of my mediocrity with your kind intercessions, so that, protected by the intercessions of your prayers, I may deserve to reach the port of salvation and obtain forgiveness for my sins in this earthly prison, as I have already requested through our brother Denewald, the bearer of my letters, in the past year. Therefore, the transmission of these humble gifts accompanies this note, directed not so much by worthy intent as by devoted mind. Similarly, I beseech you to deign to send me some works or prose, or verses, or rhythmic compositions of Bishop Aldhelm for the consolation of my pilgrimage, and by some words of your kindness, indicate what your fraternity can accomplish regarding these prayers, which I eagerly strive to hear. I wish you well and prosperous days, and I hope for your intercession for me for a long time.

It is said that Agathocles dined with clay.
And often burdened the Samian with mud.
When he placed dishes with gemmed golden vessels,
And mixed wealth and poverty together.
To the one asking the reason he replied: I am the king
Of Sicily, born of a potter.
Reverently consider fortune, whoever suddenly
Advances from a humble place.

2

LETTER II

LULLUS TO INGALICE.
Year of Our Lord 752.

To the illustrious and most beloved minister of God, Lullus Ingalice, your unworthy priest, yet in all things a devoted servant in the Lord, I wish you a desirable greeting.

Indeed, the letters of your wisdom and the gifts of your generosity have reached me, which, having been carefully read and considered, after the preceding peaceful greeting, if I understood well, you have indicated to us various troubles and tribulations that often beset the servants of Christ in this world according to the Apostle's sentiment: All who desire to live godly in Christ Jesus will suffer persecution; and against all temptations, you humbly requested our prayers, whatever they may be; which our entire congregation has diligently sought to offer to the Lord for your safety, and now, most beloved deacon, because I could not adequately repay the debt of your writings in response due to the smallness of my intellect, I know that true charity bears all things. These few words of my rusticity, along with the smallest gifts, namely, four knives made according to our custom, a silver comb, and one cloth, I have taken care to send through your faithful bearer, our brother Aldred, only for the memory of charity. I ask your fraternity to receive these with the same spirit in which they are sent from me. But also, our entire band of brothers desires to greet our intercessor before God, the venerable Bishop Boniface, in the love of God.

3

LETTER III

LULLUS TO LEOBGYTHA.
Around the year of Our Lord 752.

    To the dearest sister in Christ, Leobgytha, Lullus, a humble servant under the authority of Lord Boniface, sends greetings in the Lord.

    I do not forget your industriousness, valuing the evangelical sentiment which says: Blessed are the poor in spirit, for theirs is the kingdom of heaven. That poverty must be borne patiently, as the same evangelist testifies, who says: In your patience you will possess your souls. Retaining that of David with the heart, because according to the multitude of your sorrows the consolations of God have gladdened your soul. Do not think of your sincere dedication in the Lord as contemptible or forgotten, although we may be separated by the interval of time; nor do I in any way admit to being weary in your necessities, but know that I am only preoccupied by the cunning of diabolical fraud and wearied by the insidious persecution of his ministers; and, according to the prophet's saying: I am weary of my life because of the children of iniquity. However, whatever is lacking for your needs, indicate through Deacon Gundwin that he should not grow weary in my labors, for it is very rare that anyone wishes to share my tribulations with me. Farewell in the Lord, interceding for me as much as I am weighed down by greater distress.

4

LETTER IV

LULLUS TO GREGORY.
Year of Our Lord 752.

To the shining lamp of the Church of Christ, my most devoted helper in the doctrine of divine law, Gregory, honored with the double dignity of priest and abbot, decorated with the preceding support of his own merits, Lullus, the last of the orthodox mother, namely the Church, a pupil, in unfading charity, in the cornerstone of both testaments, sends salvific greetings.

The gifts of your generosity have been delivered to me by Fido the pregnant one, but the most pleasant greetings of your benevolent charity accompanied every gift, overcoming all in the usual manner. Upon hearing and receiving these, I first gave abundant thanks to God, the most pious, as was fitting; and then I rendered due thanks to your fraternity, because I knew you to be faithful in a lesser power, and I quickly proved you to be even more faithful in a greater one. Therefore, having discovered the success of your prosperity, my sickly spirit acted in both ways: it rejoiced at the ascension of a dear companion but was saddened by the division, for this seems intolerable among men, when one who is loved more than others is suddenly taken away, although I know for certain that no spaces of the earth can divide those whom true love for Christ binds with an unbroken bond of brotherhood, as God is my witness, lest I seem to flatter you deceitfully, for I love you, Father, as much as the capacity of my mind allows, with the affection of my heart. However, I humbly beseech you, supported by this prayer, that we never allow the charity begun in Christ to grow cold in our hearts due to the sloth of negligence, like a small spark suffocated by the fine ashes of a weak fire, lest we become a derision to those passing by who consider the building we have begun. Scripture says: "He who perseveres to the end will be saved," nor is any craftsman praised for a work begun, but for a perfect one. Know that, despite my mediocrity, however much younger in age, lesser in rank, and inferior in knowledge, without any doubt or scruple, I have preserved and will preserve. As for the gravity of your life and the stability of your mind, I do not doubt at all. Let us arm ourselves with spiritual armor according to the Apostle's command: "Praying for one another that we may be saved, for the prayer of a righteous person is powerful and effective," as James testifies, before God; and let us attend to this all the more diligently, as we are not unaware of being assailed by various darts of temptation. The stronger right hand does not cease to assist the weaker left; and the left serves the right, like a maidservant to her mistress. That is, by correcting, admonishing, and guiding my instability with the examples of your good life, although absent in body, yet present in spirit, as is your custom, do not cease to lead me to the perfection of a better life, and I will offer you, with humble devotion, as much faithful service in all things as my strength allows. I beseech you that my words of encouragement, however foolish and superfluous they may seem, are not received with annoyance by your charitable community, which alone required writing without a dictating subject, which conquers all, as it is written: "Love conquers all," and let us yield to love, having removed all pride of arrogance. These are the persuasive words that I cannot say without danger to myself, so that in this temporal power and earthly dominion, which you now possess by God's grace, you may always remember the resonant words of the Lord: "My kingdom is not of this world;" and that of the Apostle: "Do not love the world or the things in the world." What else is implied by these words, except that we understand Him to have said openly: "Do not fix the eye of your mind on that which you see daily falling by its own ruin, but look with all the intention of your mind upon Him, and love Him with all your strength, who is before all ages, and remains immutable through all ages, who has no future or past time, but is always essentially being." For what is the fleeting happiness of this world, and the transient prosperity, except vapor and smoke? Does anyone among the learned not know that there is a great distance between temporal prosperity and eternal happiness? Therefore, let us learn to enjoy this temporal power besides eternal happiness, in comparison to which everything else becomes worthless to us. Let us disdain precious garments, horses fed on barley, hawks, and falcons with curved claws, barking dogs, the drunkenness of jesters, exquisite delicacies of food and drink, and the weights of shining silver and gold, lest there be a soft resting place on cushions, and soft pillows be offered by men rather than by fiery maidens. Above all, let the careless familiarity with foreign women be cut off, for we are often seduced by careless security worse than by open temptation. Let the tumultuous multitude of ministers expel the clandestine words of divine Scriptures, for that pit must be avoided with all caution, through which we see many have fallen into miserable ruin. For often a robust soldier is attacked all the more fiercely by the most dangerous darts of weapons, the more invincible he seems. Although I know that you have undertaken this task with a clear intention of winning souls and in the zeal of serving God more abundantly, remember that a hard handle irritates a soft hand. Therefore, dear colleague, long ago, and now pious teacher, remember your last things in all your works, and you will not sin eternally. However, the haste to come to you, due to the manifold tribulation that we endure continuously, thanks be to God, has been denied to me on all sides. Do not focus on the magnitude of this gift, but rather gaze upon the devoted mind of the one directing it. Trusting in the confidence of our long-standing friendship, I wish to briefly touch upon a certain sentiment often expressed among us, when we communally explored the clear words of God, yet not pertaining in any way to your pure religious person, of whom you remember well when read, but rather to a certain most wicked schismatic, who was always accustomed to swear that he would accept nothing earthly. When suddenly, out of the blue, like a new phantom, the bishop appeared, I will greatly fear that this will now be mostly the case.

The length of a longer discourse should not cause weariness to the reader (for the wise use few words, while the foolish are fatigued by many, as I am), I beseech you, cleanse the rust of that letter by correcting it, and grant indulgence for my error. May God graciously inspire you in what pertains to your salvation; and may the Pastor of pastors keep you safe with the flock entrusted to you. I have written this with my own hand. Observe what is commanded, and you will be safe.

5

LETTER V

LULLUS TO DENEARDO AND OTHERS.
Year of our Lord 755.

To my dearest sons Denehardo, Eanbertho, Winberto, Sigeherio, Sigewaldo, Lullus the bishop, greetings in the Lord.

We admonish you to ask all who serve God everywhere, both the servants of God and the handmaidens of Christ in the province of Thuringia, and the entire people, to collectively beseech the mercy of the Lord, so that we may be freed from the impending scourge of rain; that is, let them abstain from all meat for one week, and from all drink in which there is honey; on Monday, Wednesday, and Friday let you fast until evening; and let each of the servants of God and the holy women sing fifty psalms every day during that week, and you, priests, remember to celebrate those masses which are usually held for tempests. We have sent you the names of the lord Roman bishop, for whom each of you shall sing thirty masses and those psalms, and fast according to our constitution. Similarly, for two laymen named Megenfrido and Rabano, each of you shall sing ten masses. Farewell in the Lord always.

6

LETTER VI

ALREDUS AND OSGIVA TO LULLO.
Year of our Lord 755.

King Alredus and Queen Osgiva to Lullo, the venerable bishop, united to us in perpetual friendship in Christ, greetings.

We have received the writings of your blessedness together with the assigned gifts with due reverence of gratitude, and we give great thanks to Almighty God that He has preserved you in such a long pilgrimage and in the struggles of Christ; and therefore, as the venerable men return, we signify our joy with the testimony of sacred witnesses, and we ask that your episcopate may deign to devote its study and prayer to our salvation. We also, together with the names of our friends and relatives, which are subscribed here, ask that you keep them in the custody of your letters, and that we be commended to the perpetual patronage of God through prayers and celebrations of masses. In the same way, concerning you and the names reported to us, we will take care to do as per your request, so that they may be commended in all our monasteries subject to our authority, and presented to God daily through the support of prayers. And know that it has been pleasing to our piety that your sanctity is concerned about the disturbance of the Churches or the people, which we believe has been provided for by some divine counsel. We also, dearest brother, beseech you in our legations to your most glorious lord, King Carl, to consult and assist, so that peace and friendship, which befit all, may be firmly established between us. May divine majesty deign to preserve you who are laboring tirelessly for the Church of Christ.

We have added small gifts to your dignity, namely twelve cloaks, with a larger golden ring as a gift for the dowry.

7

LETTER VII

PIPPINUS TO LULLO.
Year of our Lord 755.

Pippinus, by the grace of God, king of the Franks, a distinguished man, to the holy lord Father Lullo, bishop.

We know that your holiness is aware of the kind of piety and mercy God has shown this present year in this land. He has given tribulation for our sins; after great tribulation, however, He has granted marvelous consolation, or an abundance of the fruits of the land, which we now have. Therefore, for this reason, and for other causes, we need to give thanks to Him, because He has deigned to comfort His servants through His mercy. Thus it seems to us that, without a fast being prescribed, each bishop should hold litanies in his parish, not with fasting, but only in praise of God, who has given us such abundance, and let each person do their alms and feed the poor. And so, let you foresee and arrange according to our word, that each person, whether they want to or not, may give their tithe. Farewell in Christ.

8

LETTER VIII

MAGINGOZ TO LULLO.
Year of our Lord 755.

    To the magnificent priest of Christ, embracing with reverence and love not insignificantly, Lullo, bishop Magingoz, servant of the servants of God, eternal greetings in the Lord.

    The truth is declared by the testimony of the Scriptures that the Lord is the Savior, and it has been said about Him through the prophet: "Seek His face always." For this reason, we greatly desire to receive from your dignity the solution to some question that is indeed not easy for our weak understanding. Therefore, the institution of Christian marriage in joining or separating seems to be arranged by our Fathers with such diversity that hardly a single comparable opinion of theirs is clear to our smallness. For Isidore and Jerome seem to affirm together that an adulteress should not be held by the husband to whom she is joined, if she joins another, like a harlot, since by dividing one flesh nefariously, she has rendered herself unworthy and alien to the honor of marriage divinely instituted, and this is commanded and permitted by the Savior, when He commanded that a wife should not be dismissed except for the cause of fornication. Augustine, however, after having long discussed the same opinion of the

Savior, does not offer anything of clear elucidation, certainly graspable by our weakness; but he says at the end that how this command of the Savior should be understood remains a very laborious question, and he recalls that the woman freed by the Lord from the accusation of the Jews is said: "It is not wrong for a man to reconcile with a woman even if she has fallen into adultery." Blessed Pope Leo, indeed, says that a woman, whose husband has been captured by enemies, may innocently be joined to another if her husband is thought to be lost, and if the former returns, he says she should be restored from the latter; where it seems noteworthy that he immediately grants the right to marry to the deserted wife. According to Isidore or Jerome, the betrayal of the marital bond separates marriage. What, therefore, remains for a spouse whom solitude torments, if the decree of Isidore, Jerome, and Leo is justly believed to be upheld, except that he may join himself in marriage to another, I confess I do not know. Therefore, we beseech your dignity, by the charity by which Christ the Lord is always proven to join His members to Himself, that you may deem it worthy to illuminate our ignorance and doubt, so that you may merit to hear from the eternal rewarder: "Well done, good servant," etc.

9

LETTER IX

TO LULLO OF MAGINGOZ.
Around the year of our Lord 755.

To the most reverend Lord Lullo, Bishop of Magingoz, a humble supplicant in the Lord wishes eternal happiness.

Your wisdom surely knows that against the greatest dangers, assistance and solid methods from every side are needed. We wish to make known to your venerable charity that we are anxiously awaiting the outcome of our sister, who is at the point of giving up her last breath, being overwhelmed by sorrows and fears from every side, namely, the death of her flesh, as if erasing her own by the instinct of natural condition, and for the uncertain fate of her soul, known only to the most merciful judge, and moreover, for the tender family of that place, and almost, without any firmness of counsel, fearing the division, or (which is most serious) the destruction of souls. Therefore, humbly supplicating your greatness, we beseech you through Christ the Savior and the resurrection of the dead, that you may believe what is most salutary to be done for us afflicted by the aforementioned torments regarding what should be done after her death for the stability of the little monastery, as you may be able to gather, do not disdain to indicate by this messenger. For, as you know, there are veiled daughters of our brother there, upon whom perhaps the intention of the ignorant has turned; but none of these can yet be judged as suitable to bear such a burden, either by age or by any firmness of sense. And we fear the thoughtless dispersion of the family, unless order and stability are quickly established through the abbess. Nor do we believe we can find within the cell, or internally, a means by which they may be able to cohere, except for the little girls we have mentioned, who, facing great danger, and perhaps persuading us, we fear. Therefore, through repeated supplication by Christ the Savior, we beseech you to believe that what is most healthful can be done among such necessities (do not disdain to reveal to us with the speed we mentioned, nor be burdened).

We wish your blessedness to be well and to progress more and more in Christ, interceding for us with whole and certain efforts of the heart, in the office of Bishop Lullo.

10

LETTER X

LULLUS TO THE POPE
Around the year of our Lord 755.

    Holy and regular canonical institutions, confirmed by the authority of our venerable bishops as well as by our lord King Pipin and his advisors, we know must be preserved with manifest reason. Therefore, we do not dare to conceal from your charity that in our parish, against canonical law, a certain presbyter named Willefrid was brought in, ordained in another parish, without the consent of my predecessor, the holy Archbishop Boniface, nor of me, his successor, who, despising the decrees of your institution, disregarded our authority while established in our parish. For, knowing the authority of the canons, you have decreed that all presbyters who are in the parish must be under the authority of the bishop, and that none of them should presume to baptize or celebrate Mass in his parish without the bishop's command, and that all presbyters should convene at the council of the bishop: all these things the aforementioned presbyter, named Enred, has despised; and therefore, according to what you have defined, he has received from me the sentence of reprimand. But since he did not even wish to repent of his past wrongdoings, he was most recently excommunicated by me according to your canonical institution, and from then on he was received and defended by the aforementioned Willefrid. Your charity, therefore, should now judge what is right and just regarding these matters, not only concerning these but also regarding all that he has committed through wicked living and which is manifestly found here. For he has taken away bondsmen and servants from the churches entrusted to him, our servant Faegenolph and his two sons Raegenolph and Amanolph, and his wife Leobthruthe, and his daughter Amalthruthe; he delivered them to Saxony, against one horse, to a man named Huelp, who himself led them to Saxony. Moreover, he transmitted Willefrid, the son of the aforementioned Regenolphe, across the sea with Enred, and he gave him to his mother into servitude. However, the servant and maid whom Aohtrich gave to our churches for the soul of his son, the aforementioned Willefrid took away and seized stealthily. The name of the servant is Thecdo, and the name of his wife is Aotlind; indeed, our servant Liudo, Enred the presbyter delivered to the boy Aldbercht of Effernace, named Upbit, against one horse; and Erpwine stealthily took our servant at night, with ninety-four pigs, whom Hredun had given to our church; and at another time, he took away two of our servants, Zeitolf and Zeizhelm, and first four of our oxen, then three, and lastly eight cows with seven bulls. Moreover, the seven best animals of four years of age, which Wenilo gave to the churches, the aforementioned Willefrid took away, and many other horses raised there, which he sent to Hamulanburg. Concerning the gold and silver that Regenthryth, the daughter of Athuolph, gave to our churches, Enred took away two golden armlets and five golden seals worth three hundred solidi, and the values of other faithful men and women from the aforementioned churches, not only in gold and silver but also in clothing, arms, and horses. But since it is lengthy to recount in order all that has been taken from the aforementioned churches and plundered, and what has been done against canonical institutions, we submit these matters to your most holy judgment for correction.

11

LETTER XI

LULLUS TO OSWITHA.
Around the year of our Lord 755.

Lullus, a small and humble bishop of Svithan and its subjects.

It is the apostolic command, Oswitha, that we diligently tend to the Lord's flock, lest it perish, found outside the fold, by the bites of wolves. Indeed, I had thought that you, confident in having done this and in doing so, would act according to the regular life discipline you received from the most holy man Boniface, martyr of Christ, and his disciples, in accordance with your understanding; but (which I am compelled to say with sadness and sorrow) you are found to have acted very differently, as you, neglecting the souls for whom Christ died, of which you will have to give an account on the day of judgment before the tribunal of Christ, have permitted the sacredly cloaked women N. and N. to go freely into a distant region, against the statutes of the canons and the discipline of the holy rule, without my permission and counsel, and to the injury of God and His mother, the blessed Mary ever virgin, whose service they ought to have rendered, into the snare of the devil, for the sake of fulfilling the arrogance and pleasures of laymen, to the perdition of their souls, not recalling that evangelic saying: If the blind leads the blind, both fall into a pit. And that: The soul that sins shall die. But lest you perhaps disregard this my admonition, I will strike you with apostolic words, which say: Reprove those who sin before all, that the rest may have fear. Know that for such folly you are excommunicated with all yours who have perpetrated this guilt by consenting to negligence, until you amend this fault with worthy satisfaction. Moreover, do not receive those aforementioned wandering and disobedient women within your cell, but let them sit outside the monastery, excommunicated from the Church of Christ, doing penance, while they come, in bread and water, and you likewise abstaining from all meat and from all drink that is sweetened with honey, knowing that if you despise this reprimand, you despise Him who was sent by God to save sinners, that is Christ, who said in the Gospel: He who despises you despises me, and he who despises me despises Him who sent me, that is, God the Almighty Father. We hope in Christ that you will turn to better things.

12

LETTER XII

CUTHBERT TO LULLUS.
Around the year of our Lord 756.

To the most reverend brother and dearest in the love of Christ, Lullus, co-bishop, as well as to your cooperators, the bishops and priests of God, whose names are held in the book of life, Cuthbert, servant of the servants of God, with other co-presbyters of Christ and presbyters or abbots, eternal prosperity and peace in the Lord.

Let us therefore take advantage, dearest ones, with the most sincere intention before God and His chosen angels, because whenever we hear that your love has an abundance of peace and prosperity, and the advancement of holy religion in Christ, and the fruit of sacred exhortation from the conduct of others, we are filled with joy and, fervently praying for you, we gladly give thanks to God, the giver of all good things. Therefore, when any injury is done to your religion, or any harm is reported, sorrow and sadness torment us, because indeed, just as we rejoice in your joy in Christ, so we also suffer in adversity for Christ. For the various and unceasing pangs of tribulation that you yourselves, along with our beloved Father God, the blessed memory of martyr Boniface, endured among pagan persecutors and heretical and schismatic seducers, in such a perilous and fiercely dangerous pilgrimage, for the love of the eternal homeland, cannot ever be erased from our memory; and because he, namely through the agony of martyrdom, gloriously and happily departed to the eternal rest of the heavenly homeland, you, who are the survivors of such ones, may perhaps wander among various temptations even more perilously and more difficultly, since it is evident that you are bereft of such a Father and teacher at present. And although a certain bitterness of sadness from this deeply torments our hearts, yet the groaning of this pain is often sweetened and mitigated by the excessive and new joy of exultation, while we more frequently recall, and with joyful gratitude we give thanks to the admirable or rather ineffable mercy of God, that such a distinguished one, a seer of the heavenly library, and such an eminent soldier of Christ, with many well-educated and well-instructed disciples, the Anglo-Saxon people, Britain, has deserved to publicly send forth from themselves, for spiritual struggles, and for the salvation of many souls, by the grace of Almighty God, so that the most ferocious nations wandering far and wide through the paths of perdition may be led to the splendid paths of the heavenly homeland, through the incentives of sacred exhortation, and through examples of piety and goodness, with him as the leader and standard-bearer, bravely overcoming all adversities, and happily leading them forth, which is indeed truly done even more gloriously than the words demonstrate; and in those places which no one before him had ever attempted to approach for the purpose of evangelizing. Therefore, after the incomparable mystery of apostolic election and number throughout the whole world, and the ministry of other disciples of Christ who were evangelizing at that time, we hold him among the distinguished and best teachers of the orthodox faith and we lovingly and laudably venerate him. Hence, in our general synod, where we also briefly presented other matters pertaining to your holiness, we more fully conferred among ourselves, mentioning the day of his birth, and that of his cohort martyrizing with him, we have determined to celebrate it solemnly with annual frequency, as we seek and undoubtedly believe that we have him as a patron before Christ the Lord, whom in his life he always loved, and in death, by his grace, magnificently glorified. Furthermore, as we have said, we acknowledge that we are always ready to relieve and console your solicitude, and as if somewhat wearied by the absence of a father of the family, so to speak, as well as the generality of your subjects, the servants of God, with paternal words and fraternal comforts, wherever and in whatever business we prevail. Therefore, first, to confirm the love that they have for you in the innermost parts of our hearts, let us use the words and affection of the apostle, and let us say together with the apostle: Grace to you and peace. We always give thanks to God for all of you, making mention of you in our prayers without ceasing, remembering your work of faith, and labor, and charity, and the patience of hope in our Lord Jesus Christ, before God and our Father. For that which has already been established long ago, during the life of the venerable memory of Boniface, through certain writings and through faithful messengers, we deem it necessary to recall to one another, namely, that mutual intercessions for us and for our living here and obediently departed should be offered to the living God and judge of all, according to apostolic admonitions: Pray, he says, for one another, that you may be saved, and the rest. For in this way, we recognize that we can please divine mercy, offering to Him pure sacrifices of prayers. Thus, we will find the same prospering us in adversities. Indeed, where the Lord is present, according to His promises, all adversity of the wicked is driven away. For He Himself said: If two of you agree on earth about anything they ask, it will be done for them by my Father who is in heaven. For we judge it necessary to act with keen insight, because, according to apostolic predictions, perilous times are now at hand, and the rest, which he pursues in the same letter. And since there is no need to write to you about the external incursions of calamities, which you have frequently suffered, as I believe, that is, persecutions, plunders, hatreds, and scandals, and similar things.

Furthermore, behold how in very many places the status of the Christian religion is greatly wavering, while the order of ecclesiastical matters is disturbed almost everywhere, both externally and internally, and the pernicious sects of novel conversations are almost everywhere growing; nor is it surprising, since, after the decrees of the ancient Fathers and the ecclesiastical laws have been set aside, many according to their own inventions feel, affirm, and act in ways that are wrong and harmful to the salvation of many, as it is known that it has been said and done by a certain man of great authority after the year passed. To this, however, we, as I fear, are timid and less inflamed with zeal for justice; what else should we primarily do but incessantly ask for the intercession of the saints, the apostles, the martyrs of Christ, and the venerable bishops of the Churches of God, so that in this, for which we have been called and appointed, by the grace of Christ we may be made to persevere, and that we may not be reprobate, but rather accepted, not slothful, but diligent, not dispersing, but gathering whoever we can to the unity of the Christian religion and the unity of ecclesiastical conduct, so that the ministry of our dispensation and the diligence of our labor may contribute to the praise and glory of Almighty God, so that with those who serve well and are pleasing to God, we may one day deserve to hear: Blessed is the servant whom, when the Lord comes, he finds vigilant! Amen, I say to you, that over all his goods he will set him; and to this, let us frequently recall to mind, for example, the renowned master and martyr blessed Boniface, how or with what diligence he labored in the doctrine of Christ, what dangers and difficulties he willingly endured for the love of Christ and the profit of souls, even unto death itself. And because he has now become familiar with the Almighty, let your wisdom wisely consider whether you ought to consent to his sacred admonitions, and to follow his examples of piety to the best of your ability. For as much as he has become a domestic of him whom he loved above all, so much more can he obtain greater things from him. Therefore, if any of his subjects, to whom divine dispensation once advanced him in the place of a master, dissent from his spiritual teachings or depart from the right conduct, may he who could be their defender in the eternal judgment rather be their accuser, and may the reasons from them be required by him with the judge more strictly. But on the contrary, whoever rightly follows the rule of his sacred institution and doctrine, let them know for certain that they have the communion of the Roman and apostolic Church, from which they have been directed as a legate and teacher, and then, together with it, to have and to live with all of us, both living and dead, in prayer and in the celebration of the Mass, as we have said above, a perpetual communion, provided that they do not disdain to humbly and lovingly obey their doctors and rulers of their salvation for God and eternal reward, not failing at any time, as if undevoted or deceitful, but always as good-natured disciples progressing and faithfully adhering to their masters in Christ, to the palm of the heavenly calling of God and the glory of the heavenly kingdom. These words we have written to your holiness, not as if ignorant or in need of our rustic rule, but for the sake of love and mutual communion, contesting and beseeching through Almighty God and His Son Jesus Christ, and His coming, and His kingdom, that you, O dearest, may always be faithful helpers and unanimous cooperators with all your subjects in Christ against all enemies of the orthodox faith and heretics and schismatics, and men of the most wicked conduct. For by this, you will be lovable or praiseworthy to good men, and acceptable and dear to Almighty God; and so, with the aforementioned blessed Father and your predecessor, may each of you deserve to hear a joyful voice from the judge of all, Christ: Well done, good and faithful servant, because you have been faithful over a few things, I will make you ruler over many; enter into the joy of your Lord. Amen. Almighty God grant you all to be preserved in His holy love and fear for a long time.

To the most beloved FF. and sons, Cuthberchtus archbishop, Lullo coadjutor.

13

CYNEHARDUS TO LULLO.
Year of Our Lord 756.

To the most worthy Lord, venerable, and deservedly distinguished and most eminent, widely renowned for preaching the doctrine of the Christian religion, and for a life of most excellent conduct, to us not undeservedly, on account of the kinship of our always memorable necessity, to the most beloved Lullus bishop, Cineheardus unworthy, as I fear, bishop of the city of Wentana, from the depths of my innermost affection, eternal salvation in Christ.

14

LETTER XIV

EARDULF TO LULLO

To the most reverend and dearest Lullo, co-bishop, from Eardulf, bishop of the church of Hrof, along with the son of the holy church, King Eardvulf of Kent, sincere greetings in the name of Christ.

Veracium, therefore, is recognized as a friendly and memorable custom among allies, when, due to the distances of intervening lands or regions of foreign provinces, they are unable to visit and greet each other in person, they certainly send words of greeting through their faithful messengers or even direct letters to one another, and discuss matters that are worthy and useful, so that the mind, of course, may not be troubled about what is being done regarding the state of a friend by divine providence and judgment, nor may it be afflicted with weariness for too long, nor may it groan daily under the anxiety of uncertain matters. Therefore, primarily greeting with greater diligence, through this messenger, visiting your eminence, having the desire to hear and know that the same glorious and prosperous progress is occurring in all things, we wish in every way that we commend ourselves and our dearest ones to your blessedness through prayers, so that, fortified by your sacred and God-pleasing prayers, and surrounded by the wall of your protection, we may be defended against all the assaults of the enemy in this life, which is a total temptation, and may we deserve to reach that life which is free from death and lacks an end, through your kind intercessions. We have sent you a small gift, namely one reptile, earnestly beseeching you to consider the love of the sender more than the value of the gift, in hope of better things, which is more quickly granted to those praying for you, if the Lord grants life and strength. For we are mindful of all the words that have been spoken from the abundance of your heart to our ears, which declared how much you love those who love you from every side. For what else is there for us to do, except to love one another, as God disposes and considers the end of all things, and to faithfully keep watch over one another. Furthermore, likewise, and henceforth, whenever someone from among us embarks on the paths of another life, as I wish, may he enter happily without delay, with gifts and alms, and may he often remember and strive to protect and make prosperous his journey from this side to that, earnestly beseeching that through this our most faithful brother, the priest named Laearoredus, you deign to direct your writings of piety to us, so that through these the knowledge of those things that please you may be made clear, because you undoubtedly have in the aforementioned priest a truthful and faithful legate among us; and therefore through him you will be able to reveal to us whatever, by the testimony of a living voice, you wish. We have also sent the names of our relatives, namely Irmigi, Noththry, and Dulichae, all dedicated virgins of God, to you, asking that you hold them in the offerings of the Mass and the suffrages of prayers, because we are prepared to repay similar benefits to one another.

May God keep you safe, and may He deign to preserve you in His ministry for a long time through the ages.

Aeardulfus, bishop. Lullo, co-bishop.

15

LETTER XV

MILREDUS TO LULLO.
Around the year of our Lord 756.

To the most beloved lord and dearest in Christ, Bishop Lulla, Milret, servant of God, to those serving.

After I was departing from your presence and the bodily sight of the most holy bishop and most blessed father Boniface, unwillingly and sadly, through various events and many dangers, we arrived at the land of our birth by your nourishing prayers. There, not yet having completed the full cycle of the year, a sad message was brought to us, that the most blessed Father had passed from the prison of the flesh to the heavens; if it is right to say this sad thing, since we have deserved to send such a patron of heaven ahead of us, of whom we confidently believe that we are everywhere supported by his sacred intercessions, with God's help. And although we have mourned the loss of his presence with many bitter tears, nevertheless, he who, having shed his blood, has been consecrated a martyr for Christ, mitigates and comforts our very sad hearts with greater joy, as the glory and pillar of all those whom this present homeland has brought forth, having completed his most blessed struggle, having finished his excellent work, and having achieved a most glorious end. We lament our grief in the valley of tears, remaining in this life, which is full of temptations; he, having completed the great labor of a stranger with much sweat, has reached the glorious death of the martyr of Christ, and for our excesses, as I believe, if the Lord's mercy permits, is a faithful intercessor in heavenly Jerusalem, standing joyfully in the heights, united with Christ, in the most blessed lot, with the holy citizens. I very much desire to make known to you the venerable life and glorious end of the most beloved Father. Another thought occurs to me from the collegial fellowship, and I humbly implore your sweetest charity from the depths of my heart, and as if I were prostrated at your feet, I humbly ask that you keep the fraternal love, which our common Father of blessed memory and holy memory Boniface, with the charity of Christ's assistance, has united with sacred words and nourishing oracles, not as something transient, but as a fixed remembrance in your heart, for I know it will greatly benefit both me and you, setting aside all ambiguity, if we strive to fulfill the precepts of such an excellent teacher, and that you may instruct me, the least of all your brothers in merits, in fraternal charity, to strengthen me with sacred precepts, to support me with nourishing prayers. O most beloved bishop, do not hesitate, from which I confess and promise with faithful assurance, to follow your most sincere commands, according to the quality of my strength, in all things willingly, and with firm love to maintain faithful friendship, as long as the spirit governs these limbs, and vital status inhabits these dying members, I profess to keep intimate charity with you, God being my witness, and with all my strength I very much desire, that it may be, with Christ's granting, what is written: All things were common to them. But all these things, which have been briefly said by us, if Almighty God grants a prosperous journey, I have taken care to indicate to you more fully and verbally through the bearer of these letters. We have also sent small gifts, which we hope you will receive with the love with which they have been destined by us, God being my witness. May Christ design to protect your love interceding for our excesses. I did not send the book of Pyrpyri metric because Bishop Guthbert has delayed returning it. Immanuel. The letter of Bishop Milred to be offered to Bishop Lulla.

16

LETTER XVI

TO LULLUS FROM TRECCA
Around the year of our Lord 756.

To the Lord in the Lord, venerably beloved and delightfully honored Lulla, serving in the bishopric, Trecea, a humble native in Christ, wishes perpetual health.

Recently, the literature of your almitas was brought to our mediocrity by a faithful bearer, and we gladly received it with exulting hearts and joyful eyes, especially in your holy promise, which your bees made known, that with your constant and sacred prayers, you would want to defend our fragility; thus, our imperfect mediocrity is nearly ready to beseech your blessedness in all good things with intimate prayers, with God assisting everywhere, and we also wish to demonstrate our fraternal love towards your clemency, according to our strength, as our Lord Jesus Christ teaches and says: This is my commandment, that you love one another. And again: By this all will know that you are my disciples, if you have love for one another, etc. Also, the blessed Peter, the first and chief of the apostles, proclaimed the sentiment, saying: Therefore be prudent, and watch in prayers, having continuous mutual charity among yourselves, because charity covers a multitude of sins, etc. Therefore, our smallness, if I am not mistaken, is not in any way supported by your strong patronages. Therefore, we boldly presume to ask your blessed and truly blessed almitas, that you may deem it worthy to commend us, living in this valley of tears, also resting in the most glorious foreknowledge of God in Christ, with your constant and sacred prayers to the Lord God. I too, the least servant of the Church, with a supplicating prayer to the Lord, ask that you kindly receive me with my family, the Lord God dispensing and rightly governing all things, among your other faithful friends, who am called by my own name Aldbert, serving in the office of deacon, although unworthy, so that, improving the ministry of the holy order once received, I may progress day by day through your most healthful intercessions. May the highest arbiter of the world deign to protect your almitas praying for us. Farewell in the Lord.

LETTER XVII

BOTWINUS TO LULLO.
Around the year of Our Lord 756.

To the venerable and esteemed Lullo, bishop, Botwinus, abbot, wishes you a good health in Christ.

The letters of your authority, which you have sent to us with the zeal of divine piety, have greatly rejoiced me, because you, drawn by the rain of heavenly dew, have deemed it worthy to visit me, the least servant of the servants of God, with such great faith in divine love and the gift of secular dignity. I give thanks to God, asking, with a desire of deep charity, that you may be a faithful supporter for me before Christ Jesus through the height of your holiness, and in this world a serene-minded friend, if the ruler of all things in this life judges to have me sweat longer than you on the journey, I pray unceasingly, along with all the throng that serves the Lord Christ under my condition, to bestow the comforts of divine mercy upon your soul, that you may likewise be inclined to provide assistance to me for your churches. I also send these small gifts, namely, three cloaks, to your charity, hoping that they may be accepted.

18

LETTER XVIII

WICBERTUS TO LULLO.
Around the year of Our Lord 756.

To the most holy and ever-preserved Lord Lullo, bishop, Wicbertus, the unworthy servant of the servants of God, and your well-wishing and faithful one (God knows) bound in the bond of charity.

Upon receiving your sustenance, the entire holy congregation of our monks has sung individual psalters to the Lord for you, and the priests have said five Masses for each one, that the Lord may grant you your former health, and I said to them, at your will, as you commanded us to come here for the time. But all responded in one harmonious accord that our will in all things is to have compassion for his infirmity and to expend all charity towards him as a proper brother. But if you wish, you can come in the same way as in your own house, and we, as much as we can, wish to have compassion for your infirmity, demanding the former charity. We commend ourselves in your prayers, most holy Father.

To the most holy Lord Lullo, bishop. Wicbertus, the unworthy abbot.

19

LETTER XIX

DOTO TO LULLUS.
Around the year of Our Lord 756.

To the holy Lord of saints, because of equal merits and loving him with utmost reverence, in Christ the Father Lullus, co-bishop, Doto, the servant of the servants of God, and all the monks of Saint Peter, the prince of apostles living under the rule of the holy order, have endeavored to send eternal greetings to your holiness in our Lord Jesus Christ.

Therefore, we give thanks to Almighty God, that we not only have all things concerning you prosperous, but we also unceasingly implore the mercy of the Lord with diligent prayers, that He may make your life rejoice here in long-standing times and make you rejoice together in eternal beatitude with His saints there. Moreover, although, dearest Father, we seem separated by the length of lands, yet the distance of lands does not divide the mind of those whom divine love has united in the heart. Therefore, may your holiness know that we all, through the obedience of our dear Father Dodoni the abbot, and for your love and all the concern for you, and your most devoted holy congregation committed to God, do not cease to beseech the mercy of the Lord in our constant prayers for you. Thus, with the offices of greeting, we humbly ask that you always have this family of Christ and Saint Peter in your remembrance, and that you may make your intercessors for all your friends, both bishops and their clergy, as well as abbots and their monks, or abbesses or those dedicated to God in this congregation of Saint Peter, to be remembered in your merit, so that in their sacred prayers they should be frequently mentioned, so that through their intercessions we may one day merit to reach the desired homeland of paradise. Likewise, we beseech you to send the names of all your friends, both living and deceased, through our present brother Saganaldus, by a brief directed to us, so that we may remember them in our constant prayers as we do with our other brothers. May the grace of the heavenly King always guard you. Amen.

A list directed to Bishop Lullus. May Emmanuel be with us.

20

LETTER XX

CYNEARDUS TO LULLUS.
Around the year of Our Lord 756.

To the greatly beloved Lord, and to us all, the dearest for the love of Christ, Lullus the prelate, Cineardus the unworthy, as I fear, bishop, sends greetings in Christ.

Therefore, we gladly receive the brother sent from you to us with the sweetness of your gifts, thanking God and you that you have deemed it worthy to make a remembrance of us from such remote ends of the earth. And therefore, as we have learned you wish, we are mindful of you, as much as we are permitted to do so in our prayers, beseeching that you may retain what you have begun with a faithful and firm heart until the end; although you are afflicted by many tribulations, which almost all the saints have been accustomed to endure from the world, yet with Christ cooperating and confirming their constancy, they did not fail. We have sent these small gifts, however small in size, solely in the spirit of charity, namely, a garment from our own clothing, as our predecessors used to send to your predecessors, which we humbly pray you may graciously accept in your humility and meekness.

We wish you to be well in Christ, and we always hope for your true happiness.

21

LETTER XXI

[...] TO LULLO.
Around the year of Our Lord 756.

To the most holy and venerable bishop Lullo, the servant of the servants of God, heartfelt greetings in the Lord.

I beseech you, O most beloved brother, as I have great faith in you, that you do not forget, but always with the most discerning mind recall to memory our ancient friendship, which we had between us in the city of Maldubia, when Abbot Eaba nourished it in lovable charity, and I remember this sign, that he called you Irtel by name; therefore Abbot Hereca greets you with holy greeting, and all the congregation that remains in its monastic life, because you have deemed us worthy to be remembered with you. But whoever perseveres in peace until the end, he will be saved. Farewell, beloved, happily for eternity; my beloved, chosen by God, for charity has no price.

22

LETTER XXII

CUTHBERT TO LULLUS.
Around the year of our Lord 758.

To the most desired and sweetest friend in Christ, Bishop Lullus, and most beloved of all the bishops, Cuthbert, disciple of the priest Bede, sends greetings.

Indeed, I gladly received your little gifts of charity, and even more gladly, because I knew that you sent these with the deepest affection of devotion, that is, the holy silk for the relics of our beloved master Bede, intended for his remembrance and veneration. And it seems right to me that the whole nation of the Angles in all provinces, wherever they are found, should give thanks to God, because He has granted them such a wonderful man, endowed with various gifts, so eager to exercise those gifts, and living likewise in good morals, for through experience, nourished at his feet, I learned what I narrate. Similarly, you sent me a varied coverlet to cover my body, because of the cold, which I gladly gave to Almighty God and the blessed Apostle Paul for the altar, which is consecrated to God in his church, with great joy, because I too have lived under his protection in this monastery for forty-three years. Now indeed, because you asked for something about the works of the blessed Father, I prepared according to my ability for your affection: I directed little books about the Man of God Cuthbert, composed in verse and prose, to your will; and if I could have done more, I would gladly have done so, because the presence of the past winter horrifically oppressed our island nation in cold, frost, storms of winds, and rains, for a long time and widely, and therefore the hand of the writer was delayed, lest it reach the number of many books; but also six years ago, through my priest Hunwini, who came there to your places, desiring to see Rome, I sent some small gifts, namely twenty knives and a gunnam made of otter skins to your fraternity. That priest Hunwini also, upon reaching the city called Beneventum, there departed from this life. Therefore, neither through him, nor through any of yours, has any response ever been given to me whether these have reached you. However, we have taken care to send two cloaks of the finest work, one white, the other dyed in color, along with the little books and a bell, such as I had at hand, to your paternity, and I pray that you do not despise my petition and need. If there is any man in your parish who can make glass vessels well, when the time is favorable, you would deign to send to me, or if perhaps he is beyond the borders in the power of some other person, outside your parish, I ask that your fraternity persuade him to come to us, because we are ignorant and deprived of that same art, and if perhaps it happens that one of the glassmakers, with your diligence, God willing, is permitted to come to us, with kind gentleness, I will receive him. I also delight in having a harpist who can play on the harp, which we call a rotta, because I have the harp, and I do not have an artist. If it is not too burdensome, send this one also to my disposition. I beseech you not to despise this my request, and do not regard it as a jest. As for the works of the blessed memory of Bede, which you do not yet have written down, I promise, if we live, to assist your will.

23

LETTER XXIII

EANVULT TO LULLUS.
In the year of our Lord 758.

To the desirable and justly venerable Lord Bishop Lullus, Eanvult, servant of Christ Jesus, along with the companions who rejoice with me in these places, bearing the sweetest yoke of the Gospel, in order to find rest in heaven, sends perpetual greetings in the Lord.

Indeed, our hearts were filled with much joy, our tongues resounded with great exultation, when such a man of erudition and holiness had sent us letters. Therefore, we beseech your paternal reverence of charity, that, always mindful of us, you do not refuse to offer supplicating prayers for us to the Lord. You should also know that we always remember you, if any such worthless prayer of servants is of any value before the Lord. For how much we rejoiced at all your progress, and how much joy we would have had over those things which have prospered for you in foreign lands [...] We wish to let you know that we perpetually observe this study of charity, obtained through your merits, and we desire to merit your friendship in all things, willing ourselves to obey in all things the decrees of your just will, even with the Lord's help, when, as you enter upon the way of the whole earth, and are led to the rewards of eternal life, then we intend to write your venerable name along with the names of our bishops, and with the names of all the preceding brothers of this monastery.

May the heavenly grace of your beloved paternity keep watch over you praying for us, dearest bishop in Christ […] Written on the 11th indiction, the 9th Kalends of June […] to Jul. letter of the bishop.

24

LETTER XXIV

MAGINGOOZ TO LULLO.
Around the year of our Lord 760.

To the venerable priests of Christ, with love and reverence, we, servants of the servants of God, send perpetual greetings in Christ to Bishop Lullus of Magingooz.

In a recent conversation with your venerable fraternity, we learned that the counsel of a certain neighbor of ours, wishing to enter the path of religion with less caution, had been anticipated by your prudence with a more useful consultation, which, I believe, is designated by these words as if by its proper name. And indeed, it seemed to me that the duty of due happiness and charity concerning him could not be fulfilled otherwise than with the necessary solicitude of many regarding the same matter, lest perhaps an incautious presumption should supplant him on the very journey to which desire leads. But I consider it necessary that careful provision be made as to what means or instruments may validate that pilgrimage, which, as you know, is the best [...] stability and possible, and, if it can be done, inexcusable, with those with whom the present cause is to be conducted, and that it be approved with all the firmness of reason. Therefore, do not hesitate to indicate through letters whether it seems to you that an exhortation should be sent in common discourse in one letter, or whether each of us should send a letter from ourselves; if you judge it beneficial that a common and singular note be directed from us, I kindly ask that it be prepared by your charity's diligence. If you think it cannot be done, so that it may be accomplished without any present consultation, whether from us or from the other servants of God, in a decent and integral manner of solidity. What therefore seems beneficial to you, that we may discuss this matter through letters entrusted to the bearer of this little epistle, you may deem worthy to indicate to us.

We wish your goodness to thrive and to prosper in Christ, interceding for us with complete desires.

LETTER XXV

CUTHBERT TO LULLUS
Around the year of our Lord 760.

To my most beloved and faithful friend Lullus, Bishop, Cuthbert, Abbot, greetings.

I received your letters or even gifts, that is, the woolen cloth and linen, which your fraternity deemed worthy to send to me, with great gratitude; and I am all the more grateful because I do not doubt that they were sent out of deep charity. Hence, returning the recompense for this benefit, I do not cease to have care for you in my daily prayers; also, the names of the brothers you sent are contained with the names of the brothers of this monastery sleeping in Christ, so that I have commanded that for them ninety or more Masses be made. Moreover, I have taken care to send the book that the most illustrious teacher of the Church of God, Bede, composed about the building of the temple, for the consolation of your pilgrimage, humbly beseeching your fraternity to deign to keep firm to the end the bonds of friendship once agreed upon between us, especially in this, that you may be a diligent intercessor for my infirmities before the supreme Judge with all those whom divine dispensation has willed to be subject to you.

May the Almighty Lord preserve your fraternity in His love forever.

26

LETTER XXVI

COENA TO LULLUS.
Around the year of our Lord 760.

To the most blessed Lord, and one worthy of all honor, Lullus, Bishop, Coena, servant of the servants of God, greetings of perpetual grace.

Having received your letters, O most excellent Father, I have been filled with much joy, so that I have wept with joy from the depths of my heart, considering it blessed and beneficial to enjoy the friendship of such a Father, and therefore I embrace your desirable piety with all the eagerness of my heart, and I delight in your charity, especially because, recalling the salutary precepts of divine love, which have been imparted to us, and also adopting for some time a supporter or counselor for the labors of our smallness, whom the merciful giver of all good things has, as we believe, preordained for us in you with His kind providence. Therefore, dearest brother, wherever you may call me to the domains of holy peace, I come gladly, eagerly, and joyfully, with a full heart. Moreover, I beseech with many tears that you may deign to have a memory of us, however small, in your holy prayers, and that you may always keep the promises of well-begun piety, because a glorious crown of retribution is bestowed on the persevering, and the reward of future happiness is seen at the end of each work.

What you inquired about the books being brought from the sea is altogether unknown. Moreover, the books of cosmographers have not yet come to hand; nor do we have other copies, except those burdensome with pictures and letters. I have often intended to write to myself, but I have not yet been able to obtain writers. Perhaps aided by your supplications [...]

May your sanctity be preserved under the protection of the chosen Lady, the Savior King, forever.

I know, Father, that those things which I sent for the sake of charity have not been seen by you. Living blessed by the triumphs of Christ, Life for you, an example for the age, dearest to heaven, a worshiper of Justice, a true lover of piety, defending the holy folds with vigilant protection, spreading sweet pastures in the blooming fields, carrying a hundred coming sheaves as a Judge.

To be offered to Lullus, the most illustrious Bishop.

27

LETTER XXVII

WIGBERT TO LULLUS.
Around the year of our Lord 760.

To the truly blessed Lord, and venerable in all charity, Lullus, by the grace of God, Bishop, Wigbert, your faithful servant, wishes you a desirable greeting in Christ.

With your prayers and merits supporting us, as we believe and know for certain, divine mercy has granted us favorable journeys on land and sea after we had departed from you, and we have found our friends and relatives safe and sound, kindly providing us with all necessary things, both in the possession of fields and in beasts of burden and livestock, as well as other furnishings, willingly granting them to us. Holding this without any contradiction up to today, we beseech and implore your holy brotherhood, which has always been accustomed to aid and console us, to see and consider what it would be more useful for us to do. For all things are known to you; and this and that, whatever seems good to you, I confess to have done with a joyful heart, and I have not scorned your healthy counsel in anything. If it seems good to you that we proceed to you, we believe that useful men, and as they say, good men desire to be in our company. However, if something else pleases you more, still, with our speech and counsel, if it seems so to you, they wish to visit you. Regarding this matter, let us know what you think. But why do I delay further, when your letters are coming to us, which, as I implore you, may you entrust to this present bearer of my letters. Whatever you command or suggest in them, with God's permission and life accompanying, we will gladly do. Much of our life has been spent fluctuating and neglecting, as if poured out beyond ourselves, to finally return to ourselves, it is necessary, knowing the scripture that those who sow in tears will reap in joy, and therefore we take care to pass the rest of our life with your counsel. Moreover, if in the region of our people, namely the Saxons, any door of divine mercy is opened, take care to send back to us the same, as many, with God's help, desire to hasten to their aid. All these things, which we have touched upon in long discourse, consider with vigilant mind what it is better to do, and do not hesitate to inform us with your holy kindness. Farewell.

I, Hrothuin, have long been with you; now, however, placed in writing this, reading and teaching what I have read, I greet you much, imploring that you may have towards me the same spirit as I have towards you. Greet all who love our Lord Jesus Christ.

28

LETTER XXVIII

BREGWINUS TO LULLO.
Around the year of our Lord 761.

To the most reverend and dearest brother in Christ, Bishop Lullo, Bregwinus, servant of the servants of God, perpetual greetings in the name of Christ.

Many days have passed since I anxiously hoped that, with God's favor, our legate might finally find a prosperous journey to your blessedness, because through these, namely the immediately preceding years, very many and various troubles were reported to exist among us in Britain or in the parts of Gaul, and this, indeed, our desirable intention was often hindered and greatly prohibited by terrifying circumstances, preventing us from directing some of ours to you through such uncertain and frequent infestations of wicked men in the provinces of the Angles or in the regions of Gaul. Now indeed, with peace and protection promised to us undoubtedly from all sides by the princes, we have sent to your venerable brotherhood this present brother, the bearer of these letters, named Hildebercht, recalling indeed how we had a conversation about the convention of friendship among us in the city of Rome, which we also confess to keep in every way. Therefore, I now, trusting in your blessed friendship, adopt to do as our predecessors did not cease to do among themselves, sending the sweetest words of greeting and peace, that the evangelical word may be fulfilled in us, that we may be deserving to be his disciples if we have love for one another. For this reason, we have taken care to inform you that we have sent to your blessedness some small gifts, not small indeed in charity, namely one box made of bones for the priestly office, solely for the sake of greeting and blessing, through Ishard, a religious priest, that you may kindly receive what is ours, and likewise we wish to receive good things from you. Furthermore, dearest of all the brothers, I desire you to know for certain, with God as my witness, that I gladly receive and hold fast to your holiness's love in the same place of charity and consolation of brotherhood, in which indeed the love of the blessed Father and your predecessor Boniface has always remained unshaken and continues to be perpetually deposited, so that between us also and our own, henceforth a familiar and spiritual friendship may faithfully persist, both for the remedy of our souls in prayers and celebrations of Masses, as well as for the necessities of this life and all suitable brotherly support. And to these things which I have premised, I greatly desire your love to accomplish, that indeed all the priests of God and the families of the blessed and holy martyr of Christ, Boniface, may diligently and lovingly greet you in my name, and urge for us, which we do not cease to do for them, to fervently beseech the mercy of Almighty God. As for the return of the aforementioned matter, whether through the words of our brother or even through letters, command us to be informed by your brotherly piety.

May the mercy of Almighty God protect us, and may he deign to preserve and keep your most sincere charity for the benefit of many in perpetuity.

Indeed, we celebrate the day of the religious deposition of Christ's servant Bugga, who was an honorable abbess, and the day of her deposition was the 6th of the Kalends of January. She earnestly requested me, while she was still living, to transmit this to your blessedness. And as she hoped and believed, so take care to do, because her father and patron in Christ was Bishop Boniface.

29

LETTER XXIX

LULLUS TO THE SUPPER.
Circa the year of our Lord 762.

To my brother and co-presbyter, and my most beloved lord, Lullus, adorned with the insignia of the supreme pontificate, a humble servant of the servants of God, eternal greetings in Christ.

I humbly beseech your holiness to deign to remember the friendship once joined between us in Christ, and begun once, that it may not grow old and be delivered to forgetfulness, which we pledged before God with faithful promise. For in the name of Christ, we ought to glory in insults and tribulations, and in the exaltation of His Church, which is beaten down, pressed, and worn out daily, because modern princes establish new customs and new laws according to their desires. Therefore, I implore your excellence to be a continual supplicant for the salvation of our souls. For I am compelled to depart from this sorrowful and perilous life, burdened with constant bodily ailments and anxiety of mind, to render an account to the pious and strict judge. However, I have sent a small gift to your love, namely, a silk pall of the best kind, through the bearer of these letters. I beseech you to acquire any of these books and deign to send them to us, which the blessed memory of Bede the priest has expounded, for the consolation of our pilgrimage; that is, in the first part of Samuel up to the death of Saul, four books; or in Ezra and Nehemiah, three books; or in the Gospel of Mark, four books. I ask for something weighty, but I impose nothing heavy on true charity.

30

LETTER XXX

WIGBERTUS TO LULLUS.
Circa the year of our Lord 762.

To the holy and most blessed lord, and to me always most beloved, Lullus, by the grace of God bishop, Wigbertus, a humble servant of the family of Christ, sends eternal greetings of everlasting health.

For I am filled with great joy, and my spirit greatly rejoices, having learned from some of your blessed health. And we wish that, by the grace of God, you always have it, and that you remember us in your holy prayers, by the grace of God granting, and with your merits, as we believe, aiding us, we have crossed the sea healthy and safe, and have reached our homeland, and have offered your gifts to the bishops, abbots, and your friends, as you commanded, and have taken care to intimate your words and your will according to the measure of our ability. They, however, did as they were taught, humbly and gratefully receiving everything, giving great thanks to Christ the Lord, that your sublimity has deigned to visit their smallness through gifts and letters, and promising that they will always have your communion and the fervor of your family's prayers; and writing your name, as that of their most beloved, in their churches, and declaring that they will continually make remembrance of you, both living and deceased, and promising to send their letters written, as it pleases them, and promising all that we prolong in lengthy speeches, this bearer of these letters can better inform you in words, whom we have taken care to send to you as a presbyter; believing and trusting that he is a useful vessel in the house of the Lord, whom, if he is worthy, we beseech you to receive and have kindly and honorably, since he is our friend and relative. Therefore, we, what we cannot hide, our friends and relatives do not wish to leave this year, and therefore I have sent my messengers to you, beseeching you with humble supplication through the mercy of the Lord, that both the vows and the speeches, by which I have bound myself to you, may your clemency deign to release, and through your letter, returning by my messengers, may you indicate to me what I should do. For I confess to you by God, that against your will no dignity of the world, no secular friendship, can retain me here in any way, especially since I love you above all men; God is my witness. But if it seems good to you, and your will is that I return to you sooner, I beseech you to dismiss me from the Church and ministry, to which I previously served, for one request. My friends and relatives promise me their land and inheritance, and are willing to give, if I decide to remain here with them; but if not, they must allow me to leave. And therefore, my lord, by your wisdom and understanding heart, consider and reflect on what seems good and right to you, and that, as I said, through letters intimate. For with life accompanying and God granting, I intend to do what you command.

May divine mercy deign to forever keep your blessedness praying for us. Amen.

I, Hrothuin, once your kinsman, greet you, greatly asking that whatever you find reprehensible in writing, you forgive the ignorance of the unlearned. Would that, if it is possible, and if it is God's will, we might see each other face to face! Farewell and remember us.

May the compassionate Macarius of the heavenly court keep you safe for a long time.

31

LETTER XXXI

LULLUS TO CUTHBERT.
Circa the year of our Lord 772.

To the holy and venerable brother Cuthbert, abbot, Lullus, a humble servant of the servants of God, sends eternal greetings in Christ.

Charity which knows no end never grows old, and the internal fire barely manages to contain itself. Therefore, it has pleased our mediocrity to learn about your well-being, so that I might rejoice with you in the Lord, that you may know what is being done regarding my fragility by the just judgment of God. For I am compelled to flee from this fleeting light due to continuous bodily sickness, and I must migrate to the valley of tears to give an account to the pious and strict Judge. Therefore, I humbly beseech you to earnestly pray to the Lord for the salvation of my soul. We have also sent small gifts to your affection, one silk pall. We also ask that you might deem it worthy to send these books, exposed by the blessed memory of Bede, for our consolation, not only in our pilgrimage but also in our infirmity, regarding the Building of the temple, or in the Song of Songs, or the epigrams composed in heroic or elegiac meter, if possible, all of them; if not, three books on the Building of the temple. Perhaps a difficult request, but I believe nothing is difficult for true charity. May you remain until old age with all those who serve the Lord God with you. We also commend to your charity the names of our brothers and friends who are departing from this light, which are [...]

32

LETTER XXXII

CYNEWULF TO LULLUS.
Around the year of our Lord 772.

To the most blessed and revered Lullus, bishop, I, Cynewulf, king of the West Saxons, together with my bishops and a band of nobles, send eternal well-being in the Lord.

We testify to you that, according to our ability, we are ready to gladly act on whatever your holiness desires or commands, as we have agreed with your most reverend and holy predecessor Boniface, whether in devout prayers to God or in any other matters, in which human frailty, as God disposes, is proven to need mutual comfort; we also beseech you to remember to pray to the Lord for our smallness and for the peace of our congregation along with those who invoke the name of the Lord Jesus with you. We commit the bearer of these letters, previously designated by you, to your kindness, for he has cared to faithfully obey you in all things.

Almighty God, who gathers the scattered and keeps the gathered, may He protect you with His grace and grant us to see the fruit of your labor in the eternal homeland.

33

LETTER XXXIII

AMALARDUS AND WIDO TO LULLO.
Around the year of our Lord 774.

To the Lord and Father Riculf, archbishop, whom the grace of the eternal King deigns to preserve perpetually for the salvation of many and the defense of the Catholic Church, Amalardus and Wido, and all the congregation of Saint Peter from the monastery of Horbach, presume to send greetings in our Lord God, our savior.

Moreover, let it be known to your piety that as far as God deigns to hear us, we are your messengers incessantly, and we wish to be more attentive. Indeed, let it be known to your greatness that we have sent our priest, named Macharius, to our churches which seem to be located in your parish, so that there, in the usual manner, he might perform the office. But it was told to us by the same priest that the greatness of your authority commanded him not to be there to celebrate the divine office, for we do not know if any suggestion has reached your piety from Bishop Bernarius, for the same Lord Bishop Bernarius sent him one horse to graze from our stipend, from which we must live; we do not know if this was done for this reason. Now we beseech you that, having received permission, the same priest may be allowed by you to perform the office in that place to the Lord Jesus

Christ and the relics of the saints in the usual manner, lest the house of God and its relics remain in such honor without a priest, without light and office. Nor do we have a priest in those parts who can perform that office there, except for this one. Therefore, we beseech you that such a command and permission be granted to him by you, lest for so long, as we have beseeched, the house of God and its relics remain in such honor, as they do now.

May the grace of our Lord Jesus Christ make you flourish in the present and happily reign with Him in eternal beatitude.

May our prayers, I beseech you, reach the ears of your piety, chosen of God, so that a great reward may be returned to you from the Lord Jesus Christ for the merit of others.

This work was produced in association with:

www.ingramcontent.com/pod-product-compliance
Lightning Source LLC
LaVergne TN
LVHW061048070526
838201LV00074B/5214